1

Traditional Portuguese Cakes and Sweets

Index

Introduction

All countries have good sweets. In fact, all sweets are wonderful. However, I decided to create this book to show readers from Brazil, Spain, the United States, and other countries the delights of traditional Portuguese sweets.

We have pastries, pies, puddings, excellent egg-based sweets, almond and walnut kernels, among more. Nata pastel is one of the best known internationally, as well as Azeitão pies, Tentúgal pastels, cornucopies, or sweet eggs of Aveiro.

Each region of Portugal has its own typical sweets, most of them convent sweets. These are the recipes that have emerged in the convents and monasteries of Portugal, invented by the nuns since the 15th century. Among the ingredients most commonly used to prepare Portuguese sweets are egg yolks (because they were left over when the nuns used the whites to iron fabrics) and sugar.

And as at the time, the recipes were not written down and the nuns lived in isolation, only they knew how to make the sweets.

Portuguese sweet recipes were kept as true secrets, known only in their regions, convents, or close families.

The history of Portuguese convent sweets is directly related to the country's economic, social, and cultural development.

Sweets were always present in convent meals, but only from the 15th century onwards, with the spread of sugar, did they reach notoriety. Sugar made it possible to create various "slurries", which skilled hands were able to find and standardize. The kitchen was the responsibility of the priests, while their nuns were in charge of the confection of sweets.

Sweets were considered a luxury! They represented the "grand finale" of a meal! They were also used abundantly in the celebrations of liturgical feasts and were sold as a delicacy of the gods.

In the second half of the 18th century, the end of convents in Portugal was decreed. The nuns then needed to work for their livelihood, and the sale of sweets was the way they found.

Thus, sweet recipes began to become popular and even gain new adaptations throughout the country.

Indulge in these recipes. Every page of this book is a temptation.

The objective is to promote Portuguese sweets and gastronomy, to make the reader's mouth-water, so they can replicate these recipes and delight themselves.

Also read my other book, "Traditional Portuguese Dishes".

I will show the original names in Portuguese and both the translation, will also translate temperatures from Celsius to Fahrenheit.

Ambrosia Jam

Ingredients: 1 tablespoon of vinegar, 1 teaspoon of fennel grain, 1 liter of milk, 12 egg yolks, 500g of sugar, cinnamon powder.

Confection:

Boil the liter of milk with the fennel wrapped in a cloth or gauze.

As soon as it boils, add the vinegar and let it boil until lumps form (if they are too big, break them up with a fork). Remove them with a slotted spoon and keep the milk on low heat, removing any more lumps that form.

When the whey is reduced, add the sugar and let it boil over low heat, stirring until it reaches the spade stage (the syrup runs like a blade, 117° C, or 242.6 °Fahrenheit).

Remove the fennel and then reintroduce the lumps you removed from the milk.

Add the unbeaten yolks.

Put them in a saucepan and place on low heat again, stirring constantly until the yolks are cooked.

Pour the ambrosia into small individual bowls or on a wide platter and serve very cold, sprinkled with cinnamon.

"Barrigas da freira" – Nun's bellies

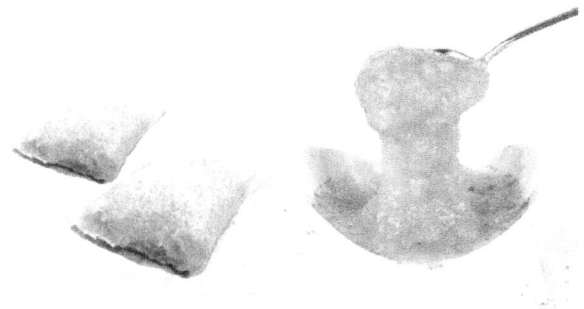

This convent sweet was created in the 17th century, and is one of the most traditional in Portugal, with several regional variants.

Ingredients: 100g of skinless almonds, 12 yolks, 500g of sugar, 200 ml of water, sliced almonds for decoration, 50 g of bread crumbs.

Confection:

Grate the bread crumbs and save them. The almond can be grated at the time of confection of the jam or bought already ground.

Bring the water and sugar to a boil and continue to cook until the water becomes pearly (108 °C or 226.4 ° Fahrenheit).Remove from the heat and set aside to cool slightly.

Add the almonds and bread to the syrup and bring it to a boil again over low heat. When it boils, keep it on the heat for a few more minutes, stirring constantly.

Remove a portion of the mixture into a bowl and fold in the yolks, lightly beaten, stirring quickly so they don't boil.

Add the yolks to the rest of the syrup and bring to the boil again. Bring it to a boil, stirring constantly, until it reaches a weak road stage.

Remove from the heat and transfer to a plate or individual bowls. When completely chilled, serve. It can also be wrapped in wafer paper.

Mother Joana's Cookies

If you want to give them a more intense flavor, you can add fennel to the sugar.

Ingredients: 100 g flour, 100 g sugar, 2 eggs, 80 g enough butter (to grease the pan), enough fennel.

Confection:

Preheat the oven to 170° C (338 °Fahrenheit). Grease a pan with butter and set aside.

Knead the flour with the sugar, butter, and eggs. Roll out the dough until it is very thin and, with a round dough-cutter or other suitable object, make small circles and place them on the board.

Bake for 20 minutes.

Honey and Nut Breads

They are typical of Beira Baixa in Portugal.

The small bread cookies we call it "broas".

Ingredients: 5 dl of water, 250 g of brown sugar, 2.5 dl of olive oil, 2.5 dl of honey, 1 tablespoon of fennel seeds, 1 teaspoon of salt, 500 g of wheat flour with yeast, 1.5 tbsp corn flour, 250 g walnuts, sugar to taste, cinnamon to taste. You can replace fennel with other sweet herbs. There are many sweet herbs.

Preparation:

In a pan, bring the water, sugar, olive oil, honey, fennel, and salt to the boil, and let the mixture boil for about 15 minutes. Then remove the pan from the heat and add the sifted flour together, mix well and add the chopped walnuts.

Return the mixture to the heat, stirring, until the mass separates from the bottom and sides of the container. Shape the mixture into balls in the shape of traditional breads and press them with the back of a fork, scratching them.

Place them on a tray sprinkled with flour and bake in a very hot oven (220° C/ 428 °Fahrenheit) just long enough to get a slight crust.

While still hot, coat the buns in sugar and cinnamon.

Fennel Biscuits

Prepare this Fennel Biscuits recipe some time in advance, as the dough needs to rest for about 12 hours. The waiting time is compensated for by the tasty cookies that accompany them at snack time. Use fennel or other sweet herbs to your own taste.

Ingredients: 500 gr. of wheat flour, 500 gr. of sugar, 1 tablespoon of fennel, 6 eggs.

Confection:

Start by beating the sugar with the eggs very well in a mixer, for about 20 minutes.

Then add the flour and fennel and mix well.

Grease an oven tray with butter.

With the help of a spoon, arrange little mounds of this dough on the already greased tray. Let it dry for approximately 12 hours.

After the time has elapsed, bake the fennel biscuits in a low temperature oven.

Milk cake

Simply delicious

Ingredients: 6 tablespoons of sugar, 6 tablespoons of wheat flour, 6 tablespoons of milk, 1 tablespoon of butter, 1 tablespoon of baking powder, 2 eggs. **For the filling:** 1 tablespoon of butter, 1 tablespoon of sugar, 1 yolk.

Preparation:

Start the recipe by beating (stirring) sugar with butter.

Then add the yolks, beating very well.

Alternately, add the flour, the yeast, the snow egg whites and finally the milk to this dough.

Grease and flour a bundt cake pan, then pour the dough into it and place it in the oven to bake.

When the cake is cooked, unmold it and let it cool.

Meanwhile, prepare the cream for the filling and, for that, place all the ingredients in a saucepan and bring to a boil, stirring constantly with the help of a wooden spoon.

When the cream thickens, remove it from the heat. The cream is ready when it looks like an egg candy.

Cut the cake horizontally and fill it with the cream obtained.

Ringlets

Also called "Christmas cookies". They are like small donuts.

Ingredients: 2 eggs, half a cup of sugar, 1/4 cup of milk, 1/4 cup of olive oil, 1 small shot of brandy, 4 cups of flour, zest of 1 lemon (scrapings of lemon skin), sugar, and cinnamon powder for sprinkling.

Preparation:

Beat the eggs well with the sugar and add the milk, olive oil, brandy, and lemon zest and beat well. Add the flour and beat well. If the dough is too hard, add a little more milk gradually until you reach the right consistency. It will be well mixed when it doesn't hold in your hands.

Let the dough rest for about 30 minutes. Make rings like shapes and fry them in hot oil. Once fried, drain and sprinkle with sugar and cinnamon.

"Tortas de Azeitão" - Azeitão pies

Azeitão is a Portuguese parish in the municipality of Setúbal, Portugal. These cakes with this form, we call them "tortas", in english are pies. Azeitão have their origins in Fronteira (Alentejo) and the recipe was brought by a family member of the owner of the pastry shop "O Cego" (the Blind), at the beginning of the 20th century.
Its production began there, first with a large pie sold in slices, and only after some time did it become established in the form of individual cakes. Although many people make pies, none are equal to the famous and well-known pies of the "Blind", a family that holds the secret and has passed it on from generation to generation.

Ingredients: for six people. For the dough: 10 whites, 10 yolks, 180g of sugar, 50 g of corn flour. Egg jam: 6 yolks, 6 tablespoons of sugar, and 12 tablespoons of water.

Preparation:
Whisk the yolks with the sugar very well. Add the flour, and beat just enough time to be well mixed. Then beat the egg whites until stiff.

Add the whites, and mix everything very well with the wooden spoon. Grease a large pie tin, line it with parchment paper, re-grease it with butter, and sprinkle with flour.

The tray must be large enough to make a very thin layer of dough, or do it in two trays. Preheat the oven to 220°C (428°F).

Pour the preparation on the tray (sheet pan), and put it in the oven. If it's electric, put it on the lowest oven shelf. Bake for approximately 15 minutes. Do not overcook, so that it does not break when rolling.

Prepare the egg jam. In a pan, put the sugar with the water to boil until it becomes a thread. Separately, beat the yolks well, and as soon as the syrup is ready, remove it from the heat, and immediately.

Add to the yolks, stirring at the same time, stirring constantly. Bring to a boil until it thickens.

Unmold the cake on top of a cloth or parchment paper, then remove the parchment paper and spread with the egg jam right away. Put cinnamon on top of the egg jam in the desired amount. Cut the dough into 12x8 cm strips and roll them up with the help of a cloth or paper.

"Torta de Viana" - Viana pie

Viana do Castelo is the northernmost Atlantic city in Portugal. This is a region of Portugal that is very rich in sweets. For example, the recipe for "Viana pie" stands out; of conventual origin, it is much appreciated in the region and throughout our country. The recipe for this pie is very traditional; it is very fluffy and creamy.

Ingredients: 170 gr. of flour, 8 eggs, 200 gr. of sugar, zest of 1 orange, 1 teaspoon of yeast, butter for greasing, cinnamon for garnish, powdered sugar for sprinkling. **For the filling:** 5 egg yolks, 150 gr. of sugar.

Preparation:

Start the recipe by beating the eggs with the sugar until you get a homogeneous and whitish mass.

Then add the flour, baking powder, and orange zest (scrapings from orange peel). Fold in with the help of a wooden spoon.

Meanwhile, line a tray with parchment baking paper, grease it with butter, and pour the dough on top, smoothing the surface.

Bake in a preheated oven at 180° C (356 °Fahrenheit) for about 30 minutes.

Now it's time to prepare the filling. Therefore, beat the yolks with 5 tablespoons of water and add the sugar. Place the mixture in a small saucepan and heat over low heat until it thickens, stirring constantly. Place the filling on a plate to cool.

Once the dough is cooked, spread a kitchen towel over a work surface and sprinkle it with plenty of powdered sugar.

Unmold the tray onto the cloth, spread with the filling, and roll the pie with the cloth. Sprinkle with more sugar.

"Fatias dos Anjos" - Angels bread slices

The name itself makes us dream. Sweet slices of sponge cake with yolks. We say they are slices of angels because the taste is almost angelic. A delicious convent sweet, ideal to taste at Christmas or whenever you want to make good use of sponge cake. Here in Portugal, we call sponge cake "Pão de ló".

Ingredients: 10 slices of sponge cake, 2 lemon peels, 2 yolks, 3 whole eggs, 200 ml of water, milk (as much as you need), 500 g of sugar, ground cinnamon, Port wine (as much as you need).

If you don't have Port wine (from Porto, Portugal), you can use a similar liquor.

Preparation:

Boil the sugar, water and lemon zest until you get a stringy syrup (Thread Stage 215° C, 234° F).

Soak the sponge cake slices in a mixture of Port wine and milk, in equal parts, without letting them soak too much. Let it drain onto a net.

Pass the slices through the beaten eggs with the yolks and quickly dip them into the syrup, letting it boil for five minutes.

Remove the slices, let them drain, and place them on a platter.

Once cool, sprinkle the slices of angels with cinnamon and enjoy.

Bishop's Slices

Ingredients: 1 cup of tea with water, 50 g of butter, 400 g of bread, 500 g of sugar, 8 eggs, cinnamon powder.

Preparation:

If the bread is not already sliced, cut it into slices and set aside.

Bring the sugar and water to the boil until you get a syrup at the stage of spade (the syrup runs like a blade, at 120° C or 248 °F). Then add the butter.

Beat the eggs and wrap the slices of bread in them. In the sugar syrup, cook the slices.

Remove them with a slotted spoon and place the slices on a platter. Sprinkle with cinnamon and drizzle with the remaining sugar syrup.

"Bolo Rainha" - Queen cake

The "Bolo Rainha" is a good alternative to the famous King Cake. For those who don't like crystallized fruits, Queen Cake is a good option, and, nowadays, it is already part of the typical Christmas sweets. However, this delicious cake can be made at any time, not just at Christmas.

Ingredients: 1 egg for brushing, 1.5 dl of warm milk, 30 gr. of baker's yeast (baking powder), 450 gr. of flour, 80 gr. of butter, 80 g. of sugar, salt to taste, 3 eggs, 280 gr. of dried nuts and almonds. For the topping: fruit jelly for brushing, 50 g of pine nuts, powdered sugar, egg threads, currants.

Preparation:

To start this recipe, start by dissolving the yeast in the warm milk. Then, in a bowl, mix the flour with the sugar, butter, eggs, and a little salt.

Add the yeast mixture and knead very well until you get a homogeneous mass. Let the dough rise in a warm place until it doubles in volume.

The next step will be to add the nuts and form a ball. Let it leaven again in a warm place for approximately 20 minutes.

Then, make a hole in the center of the dough and rotate it until you get the shape of a crown.

Grease a tray with butter, sprinkle with flour, shape the dough into a crown, and set aside in a warm place to rise until nearly doubled in volume.

Then, after the dough has doubled in volume, brush with the beaten eggs and sprinkle with the pine nuts. Bake for 35 minutes at 190 °C (374 °F) in a preheated oven.

When the cake is baked, let it cool and brush it with fruit jelly.

On top, distribute several portions of powdered sugar and currants. To decorate, use the egg threads.

Baby Jesus Cream

Although this recipe does not use cream, its name is due to the smooth and creamy texture, similar to cream, with a presentation identical to sour cream. The touch of orange makes this candy truly divine.

Ingredients: 1 orange, 1 liter of milk, 250 g of sugar, 2 eggs and 4 yolks, ground cinnamon, 50 g of corn starch flour.

Preparation:

Bring the milk to a boil in a saucepan.

Wash the orange, remove the zest from the skin and add it to the milk, letting it boil for a few seconds. Remove from heat and strain through a mesh strainer after 5 minutes.

Mix the sugar and corn starch.

Add the strained orange juice and the beaten eggs with the yolks.

Cook over low heat or in a bain-marie, stirring constantly with a baking whisk, until thickened.

Divide the jam into small bowls, let them cool, and sprinkle with cinnamon.

"Pão de ló" Lot bread- - Sponge cake

This convent cake, made with eggs, sugar, and flour, is characterized by its high and fluffy dough, much appreciated by the slice or as a complement to other sweets and desserts. The name of the cake is related to the Catholic faith, being so named in honor of Ló (Lot), nephew of Abraham, saved by angels on the eve of the destruction of the city of Gomorrah by Divine wrath.

Ingredients: 180 g of flour, 200 g of sugar, 6 large eggs.

Preparation:

Preheat the oven to 180° C (356 °F). Grease and sprinkle a cake pan and set it aside.

Beat the eggs with the sugar until you get a fluffy white dough. Then, without beating, add the sifted flour.

Pour the mixture into the pan and bake for about 30 minutes, or until the dough separates from the walls of the pan.

Remove the cake from the oven, let it cool, and then unmold.

"Papos de Anjo" - Angel craws (pappus)

The origin of these cakes, like so many others in Portuguese traditional and conventual cuisine, is related to the use of eggs, especially the yolk. The traditional recipe has variants in different regions of the country.

Ingredients:

For the cakes: 1 whole egg, 9 yolks. For the syrup: 1 cinnamon stick, 500 ml of water, 600 g of sugar.

Preparation:

Start by making the syrup. Mix all the ingredients and bring them to the boil, letting them boil for 4 minutes. Keep aside.

For the cakes, beat the yolks and the egg until tripled in volume. Pour half of this mixture into muffin tins that have been greased and dusted with sugar.

Place the molds on a baking sheet and bake for 15 to 18 minutes in a hot oven (230 °C, 446 °F).

Unmold the angel craws and prick the base with a fork. Dip the cakes in the still-hot syrup, reserving some to drizzle over the craws when serving. Serve them in a large bowl or in glasses, drizzled with the syrup you made.

St. Benedict's Pudding

Ingredients: 1 tablespoon of warm water (for the syrup), 1 cinnamon stick, 10 egg yolks, 185 g. of sugar, 2 egg whites, 3 sheets of clear gelatin, 6 medium potatoes, raisins, and zest of 1 lemon.

Preparation:

Boil the potatoes with the skin on. Peel them after cooking, reduce them to a puree and set aside. Bring the sugar to the boil, covered with water, and let it boil until you get a syrup at the stage of spade (242 °F).

Add the potato purée to the sugar syrup and keep it on the heat, stirring constantly, until it boils. Add the lemon zest and the gelatin previously dissolved in the warm water.

Let the mixture cool down a bit and, meanwhile, beat the egg whites until stiff and set aside.

Add the yolks, previously beaten, to the puree until you obtain a thick and clear cream. Gently add the egg whites, the cinnamon stick, and, finally, the raisins.

Pour the mixture into a buttered baking dish and bake at a moderate temperature oven.

The pudding should be unmoulded the day after making it to prevent it from falling apart. If you unmold it on the same day, dip the bottom of the mold in hot water, turn it over on the serving plate and tap lightly to keep the pudding structured.

Carrot Pudding

Ingredients: 400 gr of sugar, 600 gr of carrots, 2 dl of water, 2 eggs, and 10 yolks.

Confection:

We started this recipe by bringing the water with the sugar to the boil.

Let it boil for about 5 minutes to create a sugar syrup.

While we wait, we take the opportunity to arrange the carrots and puree them.

To the puree we add the eggs, the yolks and, gradually, the sugar syrup. Always stirring.

Grease a cake mold with butter and sprinkle with sugar.

Pour the mixture into the mold and bake in the oven at 200° C (392 °F) for 1 hour and 30 minutes.

Unmold only after it has cooled completely and store in the refrigerator until ready to serve.

Enjoy your dessert.

Almonds Pudding

Ingredients: 1 liter of milk, 300 gr. of sugar, 100 g. ground almonds, 12 eggs, 1 dessert spoon of corn starch, slivered almonds for garnish, and liquid caramel to taste.

Confection:

We started this recipe by mixing the eggs with the sugar, cornstarch, and almonds. We add the milk, previously heated, and wrap it all up. We reserve.

Meanwhile, we spread the liquid caramel in the form of a pudding and pour the mixture into it. Cover the mold and cook in the pressure cooker with water until half full, for about 20 minutes, once it starts to boil.

Let it cool down before unmolding and decorating with sliced almonds.

Enjoy your dessert!

Recipe for 8 servings and an estimated preparation time of 1 hour.

"Trouxas de Ovos" - Egg Bundles

This one's not easy to translate, as this egg cake has many layers. We call it in Portuguese "trouxas" which is the king of travel clothes bags, or sachlet.

Ingredients:

For the covers: 1 whole egg, 10 yolks. **For the syrup:** half a liter of water and 1 kg of sugar. **For the egg threads:** half a kg of sugar, 10 yolks, and 300 ml of water.

Preparation:

Mix the sugar with the water and bring it to the boil until it forms strong threads.

Beat the yolks with the egg and spoon them into the syrup until cooked. Transfer them to a plate and set aside.

For the egg threads, heat the sugar with the water until it boils and pour the yolks in strands. Remove the egg strands with a fork to a wet plate.

Stuff the covers with the egg strands, roll them up, place them on a platter and drizzle with the remaining syrup.

"Aletria" - Vermicelli

Ingredients: 1 cinnamon stick, 10 egg yolks, 250 g of vermicelli (sweet pasta), 350 g sugar, 750 ml water, ground cinnamon, zest of 1 lemon.

Preparation:

Bring a pan of water seasoned with salt to the boil and, when it boils, add the vermicelli pasta. Let it cook for about five minutes, and after that time, drain the pasta, then rinse with running water.

Bring the water with the sugar, the lemon skin zest, and the cinnamon stick to the boil, letting it boil until you get a weak pearl stage (the syrup is thick and runs in a thread, leaving a drop suspended at the end, as if it were a pearl).

Add the drained vermicelli and let it boil for another two minutes. After this time, remove the pan from the heat. Break up the yolks in a fine mesh strainer and add a little hot syrup.

Fold the yolks into the vermicelli and gently bring to a boil, stirring constantly to thicken but not allowing it to boil.

Remove the lemon peel and cinnamon stick.

Place the vermicelli on a platter and let it cool. Make scratches with the cinnamon and serve.

Pitos of Saint Luzia

These cakes, an *ex-libris* of Vila Real, originated in the old Saint Claire Convent. "Pitos" can still be a pun, an allusion to the female sexual organs.

Ingredients:

For dough: 300 g. flour, 50 g. sugar, milk, 75 g. lard. **For the filling:** 12 egg yolks, 400 g of pumpkin jam.

Preparation:

Prepare the dough by mixing the flour with the lard, sugar, and milk necessary to obtain a consistent dough. Form a ball with the dough, sprinkle it with flour, and let it rest for half an hour.

During the waiting time, prepare the filling, mixing well the pumpkin jam with the yolks. Bring the mixture to the boil and let it cook until it becomes "road stage" (when you spoon the sweet, you can see the bottom of the pan at 110° C or 230 °F). Set aside and allow to cool completely.

Roll out the dough with a kitchen roll, leaving it a little thick, and cut into squares of about 8 cm. In the center of these, place a spoonful of stuffing, already cold, and join the 4 ends to the center (forming a kind of bundle).

Place the dough on a tray with flour and bake in a moderate oven temperature. When you take it out of the oven, you can sprinkle the cakes with sugar and, if you prefer, a little bit of cinnamon.

Curiosity:

These sweets came from the hands of Mary Ermelinda Correia, sister Imaculada of Jesus (devotee of Saint Luzia), who was gluttonous. The Mother Superior had forbidden her to eat any sweets, as they fed her the sin of gluttony. Unable to control her gluttony, the sister, who had heard about the "Miracle of the Roses", had a revelation while treating patients with eye problems, using the usual linseed compresses. She created cakes that look very similar to compresses (gauze dressings), with a pumpkin jam filling wrapped in a simple dough, with the ends folded. Thus, she managed to deceive the Mother, who had vision problems, by making her think they were bandages.

"Rabanadas do Convento" - Convent toasts

These toasts, from the old Monastery of Adaúfe, in Braga (north of Portugal), are characterized by being fried in the syrup that surrounds them. Enriched with honey, lemon, cinnamon, and Port wine, this syrup leaves them aromatic and fluffy.

Ingredients:

For the toast: 1 baguette bread, 12 egg yolks, 700 g. of sugar, water.
For the syrup: 1 tablespoon of butter, 1 tablespoon of honey, 1 cinnamon stick, 1 pinch of salt, 2 glasses of port wine, 2 strips of lemon peel, 200 ml of water, 300 g of sugar.

Confection:

Cut the bread into slices 1 cm thick.

Make a thin syrup with the water, sugar, cinnamon stick, lemon zest, butter, honey, and salt. Remove it from the heat, add 1 glass of Port wine and let it cool. Meanwhile, beat the yolks on a plate.

Bring the remaining sugar to the boil with water in a frying pan, and let it boil until you get a soft phase. Pass the slices of bread through the syrup, then pass through the egg yolks and fry them, one at a time, in the boiling syrup.

As they fry, place the toast in deep serving dishes or bowls.

Once this process is over, sprinkle the toast with the frying syrup, to which you will have added the other glass of Port wine. The syrup will have shreds of eggs, giving the toast a characteristic look.

"Pudim Abade de Priscos"- Abbot of Priscos Pudding

Priscos is a Portuguese parish in the municipality of Braga, northern Portugal. This pudding is also called "Lard pudding". This convent sweet is one of the gastronomic landmarks of the city of Braga and, in a way, of the Minho region. The pork lard gives this pudding its characteristic consistency and appearance, and the flavor given by port wine and cinnamon is also evident. Its appearance is divine. The recipe is from the late 19th century. The Abbot of Priscos sometimes cooked for the King. The Abbot of Priscos, whose real name was Manuel Joaquim Machado Rebelo, parish priest of the parish of Priscos, municipality of Braga, where he was stationed for 47 years, in addition to other virtues, was undoubtedly one of the greatest Portuguese cooks of the 19th century and of that fair and deserved fame, spread not only in the region but throughout the country.

Ingredients: 15 egg yolks, 1 lemon peel, 1 glass of Port wine, 1 cinnamon stick, 500 g of sugar, 500 ml of water, 50 g of pork lard, and liquid caramel to grease the pan.

Preparation:

Place the water in a pan and, when it boils, add the sugar, lemon zest, bacon, and cinnamon stick. Let it boil for two minutes and then pass the syrup through a mesh strainer.

Beat the yolks and add the glass of Port wine to them, beating well.

Pour the sugar syrup over the yolk mixture, passing it through a fine sieve. Engage well. Pour the mixture into a caramelized pudding mold and bake in a bain-marie for 30 minutes.

Remove the pudding after cooking, let it cool, and unmold.

Guimarães pies

These shell-shaped cakes are one of the most typical regional sweets in Guimarães. The origin of the recipe would be the Convent of Saint Claire of Guimarães. The pies from Guimarães do not have the typical shape of pies; they are more similar to pastries in the shape of a half moon. They are not pie in the truest sense of the word. The dough is traditionally kneaded by hand, with measurements taken by eye. To grease it, pork fat is used, obtained from the confection of fried pork meat, regionally known as "rojões".

Ingredients:

For dough: 1 pinch of salt, wheat flour (as much as you need), pork fat, cold water.

For the filling: 1 cinnamon stick, 115 g of almonds, crushed in a pestle, 20 beaten egg yolks, 350 ml of water, 459 g of sugar, gourd jam.

Sweet chila (or gila) is made from the gila pumpkin (*Cucurbita ficifolia, Figleaf gourd, Malabar gourd*) and is already prepared in jars, if you prefer.

Confection:

Knead the flour in cold water seasoned with salt, until the dough is stiff.

After the flour is well kneaded, spread the dough on a smooth surface and continue to knead it, turning it around and working it well, until it starts to bubble. At this point, make a roll with the dough and grease it on all sides with cold drippings from the pork lard and let it rest for 2 or 3 hours.

After the rest period, roll out the dough into stripe form, little by little, with a rolling pin. Made a piece of stripe, widen it, pulling the dough to the sides with your hands as much as you can.

Once enlarged, roll the dough carefully and form a roll, which you will grease with lard. Let it rest for a few hours, wrapping the roll in cling wrap.

Meanwhile, prepare the filling.

Put the sugar and water in a pan, letting it boil until it reaches the stage of low spade (the syrup runs in ribbons, with the appearance of a blade, 117° C or 242 °F).

Remove the syrup from the heat and let it cool.

Then add the ground almonds, the yolks, and the cinnamon stick, bringing it back to the heat until it thickens.

Remove the cinnamon stick, let it cool a little, and mix with the gourd jam. Reserve.

Cut the dough strip into slices, approximately the width of a finger, so that they are well separated from each other.

Open the dough of the slices and cover them with the stuffing. Then fold the dough, giving it the shape of pastries, and close them in the form of twists.

Place the pastries on a tray and bake in the oven (200° C or 392 °F) for about 40 minutes.

Bring a pan of sugar and water to a boil, and continue to cook until it reaches the spade stage again (242 °F).

When they come out of the oven, dip the pastries into the syrup, then remove them with a slotted spoon.

"Doce dourado" - Golden Sweet

This recipe is typical of Peso da Régua, a Portuguese city in the district of Vila Real, in the North Region. It is made with almonds, bread crumbs, and a generous amount of egg yolks. It makes a divine dessert, scented with orange blossom water. The dessert is served while still warm. Yummy.

Ingredients: 1 lemon, 100 g. of almond kernels, 100 g of butter, 12 egg yolks, 150 g of bread crumbs, 2 tablespoons of orange blossom water, 250 g of water, 3 egg whites, 500 g of sugar.

Preparation:

Bring the sugar to the boil with the water until it becomes threads (putting a drop of the syrup between your fingers, a thread is formed without great resistance). Then add the almonds, letting it continue to boil.

Separately, melt the butter, add the crumbled bread crumbs and mix well. Cook until the mixture is homogeneous with the previous preparation. Allow to cool after removing from the heat.

Add the yolks and whites beaten with the orange blossom water and the grated lemon rind.

Return to the heat, stirring constantly, until you have the desired consistency. Serve it while still warm.

"Sopa dourada" - Golden Soup

One of the most popular sweets on the Christmas table in Portugal, being indispensable in the northern region of the country. The recipe varies depending on the location where it is made - there are regions where it is made with slices of hard bread and others where the sponge cake is the basis for the confection.

Ingredients: half a liter of water, 1 kg of sugar, 2 cinnamon sticks, 24 egg yolks, 250 g of grated almonds, 3 lemon peels, 400 g of fried bread (in cubes), ground cinnamon.

Confection:

Bring the sugar to the boil with the water, the cinnamon sticks, and the lemon zest. Let it boil until it reaches the stage of spade (the syrup falls from the spoon looking like a sword blade, 117° C or 242 °F).

Remove from the heat and add the grated almonds and the beaten egg yolks. Bring the mixture to the boil, stirring constantly, and add the fried bread. Pour the golden soup into a bowl and sprinkle with cinnamon.

"Beijos de Freira" - Nun's Kisses

These convent sweets are a centuries-old tradition in Vila do Conde, to which the nuns of the Saint Claire Convent contributed a lot, which was a true school of sweets. Of the typical sweets of this Convent, the nun's kisses are the ones that have gained the most prominence.

Ingredients: 10 egg yolks, 125 ml of water, 100 g of almonds, 250 g of sugar (for sprinkling the pastels).

Confection:

Bring the sugar and water to a boil, making a pearl-like syrup (108° C or 226 °F).

Add to the sugar syrup the almonds, peeled and ground, and the beaten egg yolks. Keep it on low heat, stirring constantly until the yolks are cooked and thickened.

Let the preparation rest for 24 hours.

The next day, with your hands, form small balls and wrap them in crystallized sugar. Then place the pastels on crimped paper forms.

"Clarinhas de Fão" – Egg whites of Fão

In Portuguese, the egg whites are called "claras", clarinhas is short for egg whites. They are a regional sweet, of conventual origin, and a gastronomic landmark in the town that gives them their name, in the municipality of Esposende. A thin and crunchy dough wraps around the deliciously creamy filling, making these sweets truly irresistible.

Ingredients:

For the dough: 250 ml of milk, 3 tablespoons of butter, 400 g of wheat flour, fine salt, juice of half a lemon, sugar for sprinkling.
For the filling: 300 g of gila jam (gourd jam), 5 eggs, 60 g of sugar.

Confection:

Knead the flour very well with the butter and milk, a pinch of fine salt and the lemon juice. Knead the dough, when kneading, to be well connected.

Then place it on a plate sprinkled with flour and cover it, letting the dough rest for about half an hour.

Meanwhile, prepare the filling.

Place the gourd jam in a pan with the beaten eggs and sugar. Stir very well and cook over low heat, always mixing with a wooden spoon so as not to burn.

When it thickens enough to work with, remove the filling from the heat, pour it into a bowl, and let it cool.

Roll out pieces of dough as thinly as possible. Place in the center of these a small spoon of stuffing and fold. Cut into the shape of patties.

Then fry the patties in hot oil. Drain them a little and roll them in sugar (granulated or powdered) to get their characteristic appearance.

Gila pastries

The original recipe for the delicious gila (gourd jam) pastries is from the village of Fão, in the municipality of Esposende, Portugal. These pastries were already well known at the end of the 19th century, with references to convent sweets in their confection.

Ingredients:

For dough: half a kg of wheat flour; 1 lemon; 200 ml of salted water, 50 g. of butter. **For the filling:** 1 egg white, 1 cinnamon stick, 3 tablespoons of wheat flour, 4 oranges, 500 g of gourd jam, 6 egg yolks, sugar and cinnamon for sprinkling.

Preparation:

Mix the flour with the melted butter and lemon zest. Add small portions of water, kneading until you get a moldable dough. Set aside and cover with a pastry cloth.

Bring the gourd jam mixed with the egg yolks, the white, the flour, the orange juice and the cinnamon stick to the boil. Sharpen without letting it dry too much.

Spread the jam on a wide plate, remove the cinnamon, and let it cool completely.

Roll out the dough with a rolling pin on a dusted surface, cut into slices and fill with the gourd jam (note that the jam must be cold so the dough doesn't soften). Pinch the edges of the pastries to seal them. Fry them in oil. Drain excess fat on sheets of absorbent paper and sprinkle with sugar and cinnamon.

Gila Pumpkin (*Cucurbita ficifolia*), figleaf gourd, or Malabar gourd.

Egg candies from Beira

Egg candies have their origins in convent sweets, and in other regions of Portugal there are other recipes with the same origin, but with differences in the method of preparation and ingredients. In the Beira's region recipes, the sweets are made from egg yolks, almonds, and sugar. They are currently one of the reference sweets in that region of Portugal.

Ingredients: 5 egg yolks, 2 tablespoons of almonds, 750 g of sugar, water (as needed), flour for shaping.

Confection:

Bring 500 g of sugar to the boil with a little water and let it boil until the stage of pearl (to confirm that it is at the stage of pearl soft ball, fill a spoon and pour it slowly). It is at the stage of pearl if, when falling, it forms a slightly pinched thread, (108° C or 226 °F).

Add the almonds, peeled and grated, and let it boil a little. Remove from heat and add the yolks.

Bring it to a boil again and let it boil until road stage (110° C or 230 °F, when you pass the spoon, you can see the bottom of the pan). Remove from the heat and set aside to cool completely.

With a little flour, shape the egg dough into balls.

Bring the rest of the sugar to the boil with 100 ml of water and let it boil until it reaches the stage of soft crack (129° C or 264 °F, when you pour a little syrup into a container with water, a consistent but moldable ball is immediately formed).

Pass the egg balls through the sugar syrup and put the candies to dry on a greased stone (marble or granite kitchen stone). Then wrap them in cellophane in different colors.

"Bolos ferradura" - Horseshoe cakes

Typical of Beira Baixa, with a delicious aroma of cinnamon and fennel.

Ingredients: 500 g of self-rising wheat flour; 200 g of brown sugar; 150 g of butter; 4 eggs; 4 teaspoons of baking powder; 1 egg (just the yolk for brushing), white sugar for sprinkling, ground cinnamon and fennel.

Preparation:

Mix all the ingredients very well, and with the dough obtained, make small horseshoe-shaped cakes. Place them on a greased and floured board as you finish shaping the horseshoes.

Brush the surface with egg yolk, sprinkle with sugar and bake in a very hot oven until they are golden.

"Tigeladas da Beira" - Beira bowls

It's not easy to translate, "Tigeladas" are a kind of punch bowl cake. This dessert is a regional sweet from Beira that is especially served as an Easter dessert, but it is a recipe enjoyed throughout the year, not only in the northern region of Portugal.

Ingredients: 1 liter of milk, 2 small spoons of cinnamon, 2 tablespoons of flour, 350 g of sugar, and 8 eggs.

Preparation:

Place a glazed clay pot in the oven (preheated and hot).

Beat the eggs very well with the cinnamon in a mixer.

Dissolve the flour in a little cold milk, add the rest and then add it to the eggs along with the sugar. Shake well.

Pour the mixture into the clay pot and let the bowl cook for about 1 hour, until it cooks.

Abbot's ears of Beira

This version of the Abbot's ears recipe is from the Sabugal region, in Beira Alta (Portugal).

Ingredients: 1 teaspoon of baking powder, 1 pinch of salt, 5 tablespoons of olive oil, 5 tablespoons of Brandy, 5 tablespoons of milk, 5 eggs, 700 g of extra-fine wheat flour, sugar and cinnamon for sprinkling.

Preparation:

Knead all the ingredients well, finally adding the flour and the baking powder little by little.

Mix very well until you obtain a homogeneous dough. Cover with a baking cloth and leave to rise in a warm place. On a floured surface, roll out the dough and cut out tongue-shaped pieces, about 22 cm long and 12 cm wide.

Fry in oil and fold the dough when laying it in the skillet/ frying pan. Let it brown and, at the end, sprinkle with sugar and cinnamon.

"Esquecidos" - Forgotten

These traditional cookies, typical of Covilhã, have a simple and economical recipe, made only with flour, sugar, and eggs. In the region, tradition dictates that these cookies are made at Easter time, but you can make them all year round.

Ingredients: 250 g of flour, 250 g of sugar, 4 eggs.

Confection:

Beat the eggs with the sugar very well (about half an hour if you beat by hand).

Add the flour and mix, without beating.

Pour the dough, in evenly spaced spoonfuls, onto a greased and sprinkled baking tray.

Tap the tray on the table to knead the dough and bake in a hot oven.

"Gargantas de Freira" - Nun's Throats

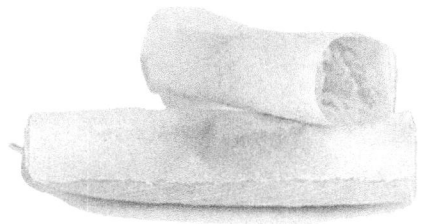

This conventual sweet from Covilhã is characterized by having egg threads rolled up, in the form of a cigar, in a wafer cover.

Ingredients: 100 ml of water, 1 cup of egg strands, 200 g of sugar, 1 wafer leaf (or rice paper).

Note: for this recipe, you can buy edible wafer paper, which is also called worker, or you can buy rice paper.

Confection:

Cut the wafer into nine rectangles. With the egg strands, make nine "straws" (cigar-shaped) the length of the wafer rectangles.

Bring the sugar to the boil with the water and let it boil until it becomes a pearl. Pass the egg strands straws in the sugar syrup and drain.

Place each egg strand cigar on each wafer rectangle and roll it in the shape of a cigar, thus forming this wonderful convent sweet.

Curiosity: This convent sweet was brought by a Spaniard named Francisco Muñoz Gomes, whose recipe he disclosed in a pastry shop he opened when, at the beginning of the 20th century, he moved to Covilhã, a city in the central region of Portugal, next to Serra da Estrela. He always made a point of mentioning that the recipe for this sweet was brought from a convent, hence the name "Nun's Throats".

"Toucinho do Céu" – Heaven's lard

One of the most famous convent sweets in Portugal. Alentejo origin. There are several recipes for "Toucinho-do-Céu" (translated means lard from Heaven's) that correspond to the various regions of the country, the Alentejo being characteristic for the use of spices, where the Alentejo cuisine is lavish. Its name is possibly due to its appearance, which is similar to that of sweets made with pork fat, known as lard "banha". The Convent of Saint Monica was the first of its order in Portugal. It was extinguished on February 11, 1881. Between 1790/92, the convent suffered an internal upheaval described in the form of a monastic history. In this story, there are references to some sweets from the convent, including the Toucinho-do-Céu.

Ingredients: 100 g gourd jam, 150 g grated peeled almonds, 18 egg yolks, 2 egg whites, 200 ml water, 500 ml sugar, powdered sugar for sprinkling.

Preparation:

Bring the water and sugar to a boil for about ten minutes, or until the pearl stage (108 °C or 226 °F) is reached.

Without removing it from the heat, add the gourd jam and almonds, mixing well. Allow to boil while constantly stirring and then remove.

Mix the yolks and whites and add a little of the previous preparation, mixing well. Add the remaining sugar syrup and almonds and stir until well combined.

Return it to the heat and, stirring constantly, remove it when it starts to boil.

Pour it into a bowl, let it cool, and, as soon as it is almost cold, pour it into a springform pan (22 cm in diameter), with the bottom previously lined with baking parchment paper, greased with margarine butter, and sprinkled with flour.

Bake for about 1 hour at 180 °C (356 °F).

After unmolded and cooled, sprinkle the "Heaven's lard" with powdered sugar.

"Queijadas de Murça" – Murça pastries

In Portuguese we call them "queijadas" (cheesecakes) not because the ingredient is cheese, but because they look like little cheeses. These pastries have a different flavor and consistency from those we are used to and, according to tradition, the Benedictine nuns said that, like "Heaven's lard", they would be the only delicacy to offer to Jesus Christ if He returned to this world.

Ingredients:

For dough: 1 tablespoon of lard, 2 tablespoons of water, 1 pinch of salt, 3 eggs, 300 g of flour. **For the filling:** 1 spoon of powdered cinnamon, 12 egg yolks, 1 kg of gourd jam, 250 g of almonds, and 300 g of sugar for sprinkling.

Preparation:

Sift the flour and put the lard on top, mixing with your hands.

Separately, beat the whole eggs with the water and a little salt. Add this mixture to the flour with the lard and knead everything, beating the dough until it has enough consistency and elasticity to be stretched. If necessary, add a little more water. Let it rest for half an hour.

Meanwhile, mix the gourd jam with the egg yolks, the peeled and grated almonds, and the cinnamon.

Roll out the dough very thin and, with a glass, cut into round slices. Pinch the edges of the slices in five places to form a box shape. Place the boxes of dough on a tray and fill them with the filling, then bake in a hot oven.

While the pastries are cooking, bring the sugar to the boil with half a glass of water and let it boil until it becomes a pearl. Put the pastries in this syrup as soon as they come out of the oven and let them dry.

Once cool, brush the surface with the syrup, rubbing the brush so the sugar becomes opaque.

Arouca Egg Nuts

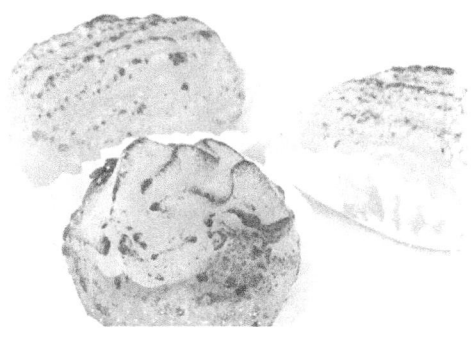

They do not contain nuts but have the appearance of a walnut. The history of these sweets, also known as "Sweet Chestnuts of Arouca", is closely linked to the Bernardina nuns of Arouca convent, who created the recipe. Like the other convent sweets, the recipe is linked to liturgical feast days, which, in the specific case of this convent, include Christmas, Easter, and the Feast of Queen Saint Mafalda.

Ingredients: 150 ml of water, 16 egg yolks, 350 g of sugar, 375 g of almond kernels, flour for tender.

Confection:

Chop the almonds and set them aside.

Bring the sugar and water to the boil, letting it boil until the syrup reaches the stage of pearl (dipping a spoon in the syrup, when you lift it, a resistant thread falls out, with a ball at the end that resembles a pearl).

Add the chopped almonds and let it boil for a few minutes.

Remove from heat, set aside to cool, and then add 15 beaten egg yolks.

Bring to a boil again, stirring constantly, until it forms a soft crack (110° C or 230 °F, when you pass the spoon, you can see the bottom of the pan). Place the candy on a surface and, with a little flour, remove pieces and tent them in the shape of chestnuts.

Place on a baking sheet, brush with the remaining beaten egg yolk, and bake for a few minutes in a hot oven (240 °C, 464 °F).

Serve them in the traditional way, in cardboard or metal cupcake molds.

"Brisas do Tâmega" - Tâmega breezes

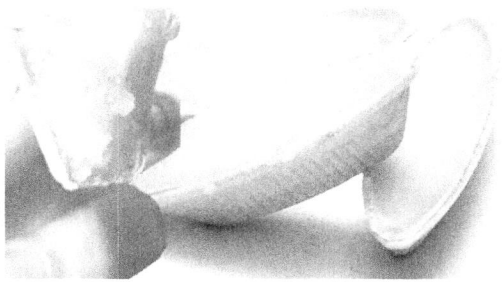

"Brisas" (breezes) are gentle winds. These regional sweets from Amarante, from convent sweets, are shaped like little boats filled with egg and almond crumbs. The breezes were created by the Clarisse nuns in the wise and intelligent use of the egg yolks.

Ingredients: 12 eggs, 300 g of almond kernels, 1 glass of Port wine, 300 ml of water, 500 g of sugar, enough dough (for lining moulds).

Confection:

Boil the sugar with the water until it reaches the stage of pearl (108° C or 226 °F).

Mix the syrup with the eggs, with the ground almonds and the Port wine (or similar liquor). Line small shapes suitable for this purpose with dough and fill them with the filling.

Place it in the oven on low heat and cook for about 15 minutes.

"Foguetes de Amarante" - Amarante Foguetes

In this case, "foguetes" (rockets) refers to party fireworks and the candy aspect. The "foguetes" recipe, like many other delicacies of conventual sweets, Amarantine, was born in the kitchen of the Saint Claire Convent, founded in the 13th century. The delicious recipes for convent sweets created by the Clarisse nuns crossed the convent doors at the end of the 19th century, and the tradition is still alive today, delighting everyone who tastes these sweets.

Ingredients: 250 g of sugar plus 250 g for the syrup, 125 g of almonds, 2 eggs, 7 yolks, wafer leaves (or edible paper).

Confection:

Bring the sugar to the boil with a little water and let it boil until it reaches the stage of spade (242 °F, the syrup runs from the spoon in a long line).

Add the peeled and grated almonds and cook until thickened. Remove it from the heat and, after cooling, add the eggs. Stir thoroughly and return to a low heat, stirring constantly to cook the eggs.

Cut the wafers into 5.5 cm squares and, with a cloth dipped in cold water, moisten them individually. As you are doing it, place the stuffing with the previous preparation, very cold, rolled up in the shape of a cigar.

Place the sweets in the oven with the tops facing the heat side.

Afterwards, pass them through a sugar syrup in pearl stage (the thread that runs from the spoon is thick, leaving a drop suspended at the end, as if it were a pearl) and let them dry.

Lérias of Amarante

Lérias are typical Portuguese sweets, but few people know that "lérias" is an expression of the Alentejo and means little credible stories or chit-chat talk. Lérias is a traditional sweet from Amarante (a Portuguese city belonging to the district of Porto), whose recipe was recovered at the beginning of this century, from recipes of the nuns of the Saint Claire Convent (Amarante), by Alcino dos Reis, also known as "Alcino das Lérias". Their sweetness, as well as their attractive and unique appearance, has made them a well-known and much appreciated sweet.

Ingredients: 100 g of sugar for the syrup, 100 ml of warm water, 500 g of dark sugar, 500 g of peeled and grated almonds.

Confection:
Mix all the ingredients well with the warm water.

After well kneaded, make rolls, wrapped in flour, and cut them into thick slices, which you then flatten with your hand.

Bake in a moderate temperature oven, on a baking tray sprinkled with flour.

At the end, pass the sweets through a sugar syrup at the stage of spade, and let them dry in baking nets.

Amarantines

As the name suggests, these sweets come from Amarante, a city belonging to the Porto district, North region, and Tâmega sub-region. The sweets of this territory are very diverse, especially those of conventual origin, of which the conventual sweets of Amarante stand out.

The recipe is part of the recipes of the Saint Claire of Amarante Convent, founded in the 13th century. In 1383, D. João the 1st issued a letter of protection to the Poor Claire nuns, which demonstrates that by this date, this institution was already fully established.

Ingredients: For the cakes: 200 g sugar, 200 g wheat flour, 4 eggs (whites and yolks separated), ground cinnamon to taste, zest of half a lemon. **For the syrup:** 1 kg of sugar, 1 cinnamon stick, 500 ml of water, and the rind of half a lemon.

Confection:

Beat the egg yolks with the sugar, cinnamon, and lemon zest very well. Add the flour and mix well. Beat the egg whites until stiff and fold them into the previous preparation.

Place the amarantines in the oven in very well-greased molds.

Meanwhile, prepare the syrup by taking all the ingredients to the fire until they form a weak stage. Once the amarantines are done, take them out of the molds and put them in a deep dish. Drizzle the sugar syrup over the top.

"Pingos de Tocha" - Torch Drops

This sweet is part of the rich recipes of the Saint Claire Convent of Amarante. Their tempting appearance and sweetness have given them the fame they still enjoy today, both within and beyond Portugal's borders.

Ingredients: 1 kg of egg strands, 330 ml of water, 750 g of powdered sugar, juice of 1 lemon.

Confection:

In a bowl, place the sugar, water, and lemon juice, stirring with a wooden spoon until you get a consistent mixture that clings to the spoon when you lift it. Depending on the consistency of the syrup, depending on whether it is too soft or too hard, add a little more water or powdered sugar until it reaches the desired consistency.

On a clean surface, suspend pieces of egg strands on chopsticks. Bring the syrup to the boil until it is almost melted and gradually pour it over the egg strands so that it drains and penetrates through the middle of them.

As the sugar becomes harder, add more syrup until the ingredients are used up.

Let it dry for 1 or 2 hours, and then place the sweets on a plate.

Soft eggs of Aveiro

"Ovos Moles de Aveiro" (Soft Eggs of Aveiro) is the product obtained by adding raw egg yolks to a sugar syrup. Ovos-moles are typical regional sweets from the city of Aveiro. It is a recipe made with eggs and sugar, inherited from conventual sweets, and was originally made by the nuns of the various convents existing in the region until the 19th century - Dominican, Franciscan, and Carmelite. But it is said that the nuns of the Monastery of Jesus of Aveiro created the recipe.
"Ovos Moles de Aveiro" were referred to as a royal lunch dessert in 1908.

Ingredients: 12 egg yolks, 12 spoons of sugar, 12 spoons of water, 4 wafer leaves with the molds, and egg whites to seal the leaves.

Confection:

Place the egg yolks, sugar and water in a saucepan and bring to the boil, stirring constantly until the cream thickens. Let it cool.

Pour small portions of the cooled egg cream onto 2 wafer sheets (leave a little cream to spread over the other sheets). With a knife, spread the cream well to fill the spaces between the molds.

Spread the molds from the other wafer sheets and place them on top of the previous ones.

Cut out the filled wafer molds.

Dip your thumb and forefinger in egg white to make the edges come together well. Cut the shavings from the molds and you will have sweets ready.

"Pão de Ló de Ovar" - Ovar sponge cake

This cake is considered the *ex-libris* of the city of Ovar. The recipe dates from the 18th century and is made only with eggs (especially yolks), sugar and flour and, after it is ready, the sponge cake dough remains moist (the moist interior is known as "pito"), letting its characteristic soft-egg filling. According to oral tradition, in the 19th century, several families from Ovar dedicated themselves to the confection of regional sweets, among which the famous "Pão de Ló de Ovar" stood out.

Ingredients: 125 g of flour, 250 g of sugar, 5 egg whites, 18 yolks.

Confection:

Preheat the oven to 180°C (356°F).

For a few minutes, whisk the yolks with the whites and sugar until you obtain a thick mixture, with a volume much greater than the initial volume.

Add the flour, previously sifted at least twice, and beat gently.

Grease a round shape (22 cm in diameter) and line it with baking parchment paper.

Pour the dough into the mold and bake the sponge cake for about 15 minutes. You must switch off the oven after the indicated cooking time and leave the oven door open (but without removing the cake yet). Remove the cake only when the oven is cool.

The surface of the cake should be moist even though the dough is not fully baked. However, the process is just like that because, in this way, the sponge cake maintains its characteristic humidity, provided by the soft-eggs filling, the next day.

Coimbra's Arrufadas

Arrufadas are considered the most famous cake in Coimbra, being particularly linked to the Pascal tradition. In the past, it was possible to find ruffles in two shapes: round, as nowadays, or horseshoe-shaped. They were made in large quantities at the Convent of Saint Anna (but they are also mentioned in the books of the Convent of Saint Claira-the-old).

Ingredients: 10 eggs, 2 kg of wheat flour, 200 g of butter, 50 g of baker's yeast, 500 g of sugar (for sprinkling), milk (optional).

Confection:

The night before, knead the flour with the eggs, the sugar, and the yeast previously dissolved in a little warm water (if it is necessary to make the dough more malleable, add a little warm milk).

Add the melted butter, continuing to knead, until the dough comes away from your hands and the edges of the bowl.

Allow to rise overnight, covered with a cloth.

Preheat the oven to 180 °C (356 °F) the next day before tending the dough). Then roll out the cakes, forming small balls with 4 cm in diameter. Let them rise again until they double in volume (about 40 minutes).

When the yeast time is over, place the cakes on trays, brush them with egg yolk and bake for about 25 minutes.

When they are cooked, remove them and sprinkle with sugar. Serve the cakes hot or cold.

Charcada of Coimbra

This dessert is made with whipped eggs threads and sugar syrup.

Ingredients: 8 eggs + 4 yolks, 1 glass of water, 550 g of sugar, confetti candies of various colors.

Confection:

Bring 400 g sugar and water to a boil and cook until it forms a paste (101 °C or 213 °F, the syrup runs off leaving a thin layer on the spoon).

Meanwhile, beat the eggs with the yolks.

Pour the eggs over the boiling sugar, using the funnel used to make the egg strands. When the eggs run out, pour the sugar syrup over them, from the middle of the crown to the sides, turning the charcada at the same time to prevent it from sticking to the sides and bottom of the container.

When the syrup has disappeared and bits of burnt eggs begin to appear, remove it from the heat and place it on the serving plate. Bring the remaining 150 grams of sugar to the boil and let it caramelize.

Pour the caramel over the charcada, making lines, and decorate the entire surface with colored confetti sprinkles.

"Pastéis do Lorvão" - Lorvão pastries

These pastries, created by the nuns at the Monastery of Lorvão, in the municipality of Penacova, district of Coimbra, were traditionally offered by the monks to guests and people who visited the Monastery.
The famous sweets conquered personalities, such as General Wellington, when he stayed there during the Peninsular War.
After the extinction of the religious orders, the recipe was adopted by the local people, and is nowadays available in pastry shops and other establishments in the region. They are deliciously dense and moist

cakes, with a texture identical to that of cheesecakes, made with egg yolks and ground almonds.

Ingredients: 1 spoon (small) of cinnamon, 1 spoon (small) of butter, 12 egg yolks, 120 g of peeled and ground almonds, 2 egg whites, 250 ml of water, 420 g of sugar (for the topping), 80 g of flour wheat, lemon zest.

Confection:

Preheat the oven to 180° C (356 °F). Grease and sprinkle 8 muffin tins and set aside.

Bring the sugar to the boil with the water and let it boil until it reaches the stage of spade (the syrup runs from the spoon in wide ribbons, with the appearance of a blade).

Remove the pan from the heat. Add the flour, ground almonds, and butter.

Stir well and bring to the boil again. Continue to stir. When it boils, remove it from the heat again and let it cool down a bit.

Separately, mix the yolks, whites, cinnamon and lemon zest. Add this mixture to the mass of almonds and sugar (already cool).

Mix all the ingredients well and fill the molds almost to the top (these pastries rise well, but do not overflow).

Bake them in the oven for about 25 to 30 minutes, until they are a bit toasted.

Once cooked, wrap them in sugar and place them in paper cups.

Saint Claire Pastels

These pastries are one of the best known Portuguese convent sweets, in the shape of a half-moon, filled with egg and almond jam. Their name is related to the convent where they originated.

Ingredients:

For dough: 250 g. of butter, 500 g. of flour. **For the filling:** 150 g of ground almonds, 250 g of sugar, 150 ml of water, 9 egg yolks, powdered sugar (for sprinkling).

Confection:

Bring the sugar to the boil with the water until it forms threads (when dipping the spoon in the syrup, thin and crispy threads run from it). Remove from the heat and add the ground almonds, then add the yolks, previously broken.

Bring it back to a boil until it reaches a point (110 °C or 230 °F, when you can see the bottom of the pan when you pass the spoon through it).

For the dough, start by sifting the flour into a bowl and working it by hand with the butter (by dipping your hand in cold water). Knead well until the dough becomes elastic and suitable for tendering.

Roll out the dough so that it is very thin and pour mounds of stuffing over it. Fold in half and cut the pastries into a half-moon shape.

Arrange them on a greased baking tray, brush with beaten egg and sprinkle with sugar. Bake in a medium temperature oven.

Tentúgal pastries

Formerly called "Pastel do Convento" (Convent pastel), the Tentúgal pastries, also known as "Poor pastel", were created by the nuns of the Carmelo of Tentúgal, starting to be made outside the convent during the reforms that, in 1834, put an end to the religious congregations. They are known for their very thin and unique puff pastry in the world. Currently, the pastries are known for their elongated shape, reminiscent of a pillow, and the typical filling of egg jam. Due to their shape, the Tentúgal pastries are also called "Palitos" (toothpicks).

Ingredients:

For dough: 1 pinch of salt, 2 tablespoons of butter, 200 ml of water, 500 g of flour. **For the filling:** 12 egg yolks, 250 g of sugar.
For the topping: powdered sugar.

Confection:

Sift the flour several times into a bowl and make a well in the middle, into which you pour the melted butter. Mix well.

Heat the water where you previously dissolved the salt. Add it, little by little, to the flour, kneading until the dough comes away from your hands. Shape it into a ball and place it on a plate previously sprinkled with flour. Also, sprinkle the dough with a little flour and cover it with a heated bowl, letting it rest for 30 minutes.

Meanwhile, prepare the soft eggs for the filling. Lay a cloth on a smooth, clean surface. Brush the dough with a little butter melted in a bain-marie or oil; remove small pieces and spread them, with the rolling pin, on the cloth (be careful not to break the dough, which should be as thin as a sheet of paper).

Cut the dough into rectangles measuring 14 cm x 10 cm, removing the thick edges, which should not be used for the pastry sheets.

Melt a little more butter in a bain-marie. Then overlap four sheets of dough, brushing them, one by one, with the melted butter as you overlap them.

Roll up the pastries, folding the ends up, using 2 tablespoons of soft-eggs on each rectangle of dough (four sheets).

Distribute the pastries on a baking sheet and bake for about 15 minutes in a hot oven (200 °C, 392 °F).

When you take them out of the oven, sprinkle them with powdered sugar.

"Fatias de Tomar"- Slices of Tomar

Although there is no certainty regarding the origin of this sweet, it is believed that the slices will come from the convent of Saint Iria of Tomar, and legend has it that this was the favorite dessert of the friars of the Convent of Christ. There are those who link the origin of the dessert to a Templar convent. There are many variants of desserts with slices of bread soaked in egg yolks and fried. Various regions have adaptations and terms such as "Slices of the Angels", "Golden slices", "Rabanadas", etc. Some use regular bread, others use sponge cake or even King cake.

To make the recipe, you need a lot of egg yolks, sugar, and water. The pan used to cook them is only sold in the city of Tomar, but they can also be made in a form that seals well.

Ingredients:

For the slices: 24 yolks. **For the syrup:** 1 liter of water, 1 kg of sugar.

Confection:

Separate the yolks from the whites and immediately beat the yolks (for 1 hour, by hand, or 20 minutes in an electric mixer).

Pour the dough into an oval shape with a lid, very well greased. Place the mold in a water bath, already boiling, and let it cook for 1 hour without ever stopping the boiling of the water. Check the doneness with a toothpick and, when the yolk mass is cooked, remove it and let it cool.

While the dough is cooling and before being cut, prepare the syrup. Bring the sugar and water to a boil and let it boil for about 5 minutes until the syrup reaches a weak stage (103° C or 217 °F).

Unmold the yolk cake, let it cool, and cut it into thick slices on top.

Dip the slices, one by one, into the sugar syrup, which should bubble up slightly. Let them swell until they absorb some syrup.

Carefully remove the slices with the slotted spoon and place them on a serving platter, basting them with the remaining syrup. You can decorate the candy with strands of eggs and cherries, if you wish.

"Farturas"

The name is not easy to translate; it means "Plenty" or "Fulness".
I don't know if the "Farturas" were created in Portugal, but they say so.
In some countries, I know that "churros" are made with chocolate filling
or egg cream (just like here), but the traditional churros with fried
dough, sprinkled with sugar and cinnamon, have been sold at all
markets for many decades.

Ingredients: 7 dl of hot water, other than boiling, 500 g of self-rising
wheat flour, 1 tsp of baking powder, 1 tsp of baking soda, 1 pinch of
salt, sugar for sprinkling, cinnamon powder for sprinkling, vegetable oil
for frying.

Confection:

Bring the water to a boil with the salt. Once it starts to boil, remove it
from the heat and set it aside.

Mix the flour, baking powder and bicarbonate of soda in a bowl. Add
the water in a stream and beat until obtaining a homogeneous mixture.

Pour the oil into a pan as wide as possible and let it heat up.

Place a portion of the dough in the pastry bag and pour it into the
skillet in circles from the periphery of the skillet to the center, forming a
spiral.

When you reach the center, lift the tip of the pastry bag; this should be enough to break the dough.

Let the dough brown on one side, turn it with two spoons and let it brown on the other side.

As soon as the "Fartura" is fried on both sides.

Remove from skillet and place on absorbent paper to drain.

In a bowl, combine the sugar with the cinnamon.

Cut the spiral of "Fartura" into pieces of approximately 15 cm. Dip the fillings one by one into the sugar mixture while they are hot.

Repeat the entire process until all the dough is finished.

Fresh Cheese Pudding

This pudding is one of the delicacies of the regional sweets of Tomar, having as its main ingredient the fresh cheeses typical of that locality. Because it comes from a traditional recipe, it has yolks and sugar, which are typical of this kind of sweet.

Ingredients: 10 egg yolks, 2 egg whites, 280 g of sugar, 4 fresh white cheeses (without being salty).

Confection:

Pass the cheese through a strainer or grater. If they have salt, soak them in cold water, changing the water several times, before ironing them.

In a bowl, lightly mix the egg yolks, whites, and sugar. Add the grated cheese and mix without beating.

Pour into a well-greased loaf pan and bake in a low-temperature oven for about 45 minutes.

"Brisas do Lis" – Breezes of Lis

Lis is the name of the river that bathes Leiria city. The origin of "Brisas do Lis" seems to have been, in the 17th century, the Saint Ana Convent, which belonged to the Dominican order. The secret behind the production of these sweets, which are an *ex-libris* of Portuguese sweets, has been passed down to the present day. There is only the oral tradition of confectioners who received information from older confectioners. The recipe we have is only approximate.

Based on this recipe, the famous "Quindins" were created in Brazil - using coconut (instead of almonds), as almonds are a less common ingredient there.

Ingredients: 100 ml of water, 100 g of almond kernels, 250 g of powdered sugar, 3 egg whites, 6 egg yolks, and slices of bread.

Confection:

Heat the oil over a low flame until it reaches 190° C (374 °F).

Beat the eggs with the milk, sugar, cinnamon, and vanilla. Place the almonds in a deep dish. Pass the bread through the egg mixture and then through the almonds, pressing well into the bread.

Fry the slices in hot oil until they are golden.

Drain the bread toast on absorbent paper and serve while still warm.

Monastery of Alcobaça breads

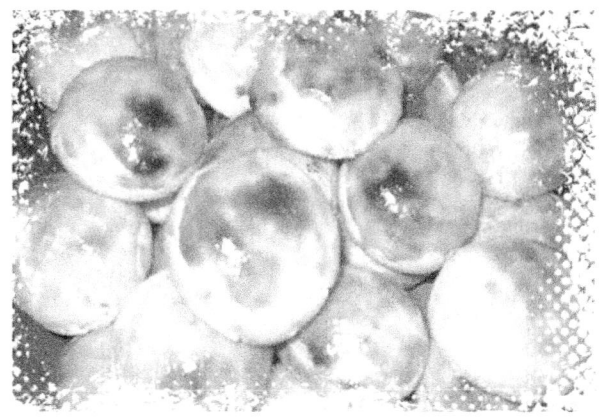

Alcobaça's cuisine is one of the most tempting in the Leiria region, largely thanks to the influence of the religious orders of the Alcobaça Monastery and the Convent of Cós, which left recipes for convent sweets that delight the palate. These breads, also called "Broinhas de Alcobaça" or simply "Broas de Alcobaça", are traditional pastries of the conventual legacy, made with sugar, almonds, flour, and eggs.

Ingredients: 300 g of ground almonds, 50 g of wheat flour, 500 g of sugar, and 6 eggs (for brushing).

Confection:

Bring the sugar to the boil until it reaches the stage of paste (the syrup runs off the spoon, leaving a slightly sticky layer). Add the almonds, eggs, and flour, mixing well. Remove after heating.

When the dough is lukewarm, dip your hands in flour and tent the breads, placing them on a buttered and floured tray.

Brush generously with egg and bake in the oven.

Alcobaça egg pudding

The egg pudding of the Friars of the Monastery of Alcobaça is one of the specialties of convent sweets that are part of the region's rich gastronomic heritage. It maintains the typical features of convent sweets, made with eggs and sugar.

Ingredients: 1 kg of sugar; 2 whole eggs; 14 yolks; 250 ml of water; and 50 g of butter.

Confection:

Bring the sugar and water to a boil until you get a paste-like syrup.

Let it cool a little and add the yolks with the whole eggs and the butter, mixing well until obtaining a homogeneous mixture.

Pour the mixture into a well-greased pudding mold and bake in the oven for about an hour in a bain-marie. Check for doneness by inserting a toothpick, which should come out damp but clean.

When it is cooked, let the pudding cool and unmold it.

Friar John's Delights

This convent sweet is one of the icons of Cistercian convent sweets and one of the most famous recipes for regional sweets in Alcobaça. The recipe is based on fruit - the most outstanding product in the region, preferably very ripe and sweet. A lot of sugar and chopped nuts are added to it, making this sweet delicious.

Ingredients: 1 cinnamon stick, 500 g of ripe fruit to your taste, 500 g of peaches, grapes, and quince, 50 g of chopped walnuts, and 700 g of sugar.

Confection:

Peel the fruit and cut it into small pieces.

Bring the fruit, sugar, and cinnamon stick to a boil, over low heat, until it forms a road (when you pass the spoon, you can see the bottom of the pan). Add the walnuts and boil for 2 minutes.

Remove the cinnamon stick, if you have placed it, and store it in jam jars. Serve on a platter or in individual servings.

"Trouxas de ovos das Caldas" - Egg bundles from Caldas

Egg bundles are one of the many legacies of convent sweets, with different recipes in the different regions of Portugal. All of them are characterized by their presentation; bright yellow rolls measuring about 5 cm, dipped in sugar syrup. Considered an exquisite dessert, traditionally consumed on festive occasions, the "Trouxas das Caldas" are currently sought after throughout the year, being an icon of local sweets. There is no exact data regarding the origin of this regional sweet from Caldas da Rainha, but the recipe may have come from the Convent of Cós, which supplied the Monastery of Alcobaça.

Ingredients: 1 kg of sugar, 18 yolks, 2 egg whites, and 300 ml of water.

Confection:

Bring the sugar to the boil with the water and let it boil until it forms threads (when there are threads of syrup running without great resistance).

Meanwhile, pass the yolks through a fine sieve and mix them with the whites, just to bind.

Once the sugar is at the desired point, remove the pan from the heat and immediately pour a small cup with the egg mixture into the middle.

Bring to a boil and, with a slotted spoon, remove the leaves that form as soon as the eggs coagulate, placing them to drain over a sieve. As needed, spray the syrup with cold water to keep it thick, and cook the whole egg mixture in the same way.

To assemble the candy, overlap two sheets, with the shiny part facing down. Trim the sides with a knife and place the shavings over the middle of the boards.

Wrap the bundles in the traditional way and serve them drizzled with sugar syrup.

"Broas das Donas" - Donas breads

These breads, also known as "Breads of Santarém", were created by the nuns of the Saint Dominic of Donas Convent, generically known as "Convento das Donas". This convent, extinct in the 19th century, was one of the oldest in the city, inhabited by nuns of the Dominican order. The breads are a little hard and can be stored for several days.

Ingredients: 1 spoon of cinnamon, 1 spoon of fennel, 1 kg of wheat flour, 1 pinch of cloves, 125 g of almond kernels, 150 ml of water, 250 g of brown sugar, 400 ml of fine olive oil, sugar to sprinkle.

Confection:

Blanch the almonds and skin them while still hot. Pass them until you get a fine crumb and set them aside. Heat the oil with the water, sugar, and sweet herbs.

When it boils, remove it from the heat and pour it over the flour in a large container. Add the almonds and beat until the ingredients are well mixed.

Let the dough cool and mold small round buns.

Arrange them on a tray sprinkled with flour and bake them in a preheated oven until the breads are cooked and golden.

Place them on a serving plate and sprinkle with sugar.

"Celestes de Santa Clara" - Celestials of Saint Claire

These cookies, made with almonds, eggs, and sugar, which are one of the best known delicacies in Santarém, were created by the Poor Clares nuns of the Saint Claire Convent, hence their name. According to legend, the recipe was conceived by the angels of heaven, who gave it to the nuns as a reward for their faith. For many years, the recipe was kept secret. But a specialty grocery store in Santarém bought it and started advertising and selling it.

Ingredients: 200 ml of water, 24 egg yolks and 2 whites, 250 g of almonds, 500 g of powdered sugar, slices and strips of wafer (or rice paper).

Confection:
Bring the sugar and water to a boil, and continue to cook until threads form (when the syrup slightly adheres to the spoon, and when you remove a little, a thread forms with which you can make shapes on a smooth surface).

Add the crushed almonds and let it cook. Beat the yolks with the egg whites.

Remove the mixture from the heat, let it cool a little, and add the beaten egg yolks. Then mix well and bring to a simmer again, stirring constantly until the mixture thickens and comes off the sides of the pan. After that, pour the mixture into a container and let it cool and harden.

Form mounds with the dough and place them on the wafer circles, surrounding them with cut strips, and bake until the ends are toasted.

Donas Convent heavenly Cheeses

We call them cheeses because of their appearance. They look like little cheeses. The Santarém region is an illustrious heir to the traditions of convent sweets from the Monasteries and Convents that previously existed in Ribatejo. This delicious recipe is an example of that, having been created by Dominican nuns from the Saint Dominic of Donas Convent in Santarém. As they are cookies of conventual origin, with their name they evoke heaven, an element of Christian devotion; the presentation and consistency of these delicate sweets, give them the name of "Queijinhos" (little cheeses).

Ingredients: 15 egg yolks, 250 g of sugar, 150 ml of water, powdered sugar (for sprinkling).

Confection:

Bring the sugar and water to a boil until a hard ball forms (129 °C or 264 °F, a consistent ball forms by pouring a little syrup into a bowl of cold water).

Remove from the heat and carefully add the yolks, stirring constantly. Return to the heat, stirring, until it thickens and forms a point (when you pass the spoon, you can see the bottom of the pan).

Let the dough cool completely and, when cooled shape the cheeses, with the help of powdered sugar. Note that the sugar is only used to lightly dust your hands in order to allow the dough to be molded.

Once molded, sprinkle the cakes with a little more powdered sugar and make some checkered creases on the surface.

Place the cheeses in crimped paper forms.

Pampilhos

These traditional cakes from Santarém are long and thin, like a cigar, and have a traditional Portuguese flavor that comes from the soft-egg and cinnamon filling.

These cakes were created in honor of the Ribatejo campinos, who use a long stick to drive their cattle, which is exactly called "pampilho". The cake was a creation about 30 years ago by Mr. Diamantino Veloso, then pastry chef at Pastelaria Acides.

Ingredients:

For dough: 250 g of sugar, 250 g of margarine butter, 2 eggs and 1 yolk (for brushing), 600 g of flour. For the soft eggs filling: 3 tablespoons of water, 4 egg yolks, 60 g of sugar, and ground cinnamon.

Confection:

Mix the sugar with the softened margarine and the eggs. Add the flour and work the dough vigorously.

Let it rest for a while, and in the meantime, prepare the soft eggs. Bring the yolks to the boil with the sugar and water, stirring constantly until thickened.

Remove the soft eggs from the heat and let them cool.

Roll out the dough with a floured rolling pin and cut it into rectangles. Stuff each one with the soft eggs and sprinkle them with cinnamon.

Roll up the cakes, brush them with egg yolk and bake them in the oven for about 20 minutes at 200° C (392 °F).

Zêzere Bowls

A kind of punch bowl dessert. Round candy, based on milk, flour, and eggs. In traditional Portuguese sweets, there are different recipes for the famous bowls, which vary depending on the region. The Ferreira do Zêzere-style bowls, in the district of Santarém, are one of the most famous recipes for this regional sweet. In historical archives, the recipe for a sweet called "Tigeladas de D. Maria de Vilhena" was found in the Book of the Kitchen of Infanta Lady Mary, published by the National Press - Casa da Moeda, which coincides with the recipe for Tigeladas de Abrantes. In an approximately consensual way, the product is considered a convent sweet.

Ingredients: 1 cup of flour, 1 liter of milk, 500 g of sugar, 4 eggs and 16 yolks, and the zest of 1 lemon.

Confection:

Beat very well (about half an hour by hand or 10 minutes in an electric mixer) the eggs, yolks, and sugar with the lemon zest, adding the flour little by little. Note that if you blend the ingredients in the machine, the bowls will be stiffer.

Add the milk, stir and pour the mixture into unglazed clay bowls, previously heated and very hot, without being too full.

Bake the bowls in a strong oven at a strong temperature for about 20 minutes.

Heavenly cheeses of Constância

This is a relic of convent sweets, created by the Poor Clares sisters, still maintaining great secrecy in the art of their confection.

The recipe is based on the harmonious combination of eggs with sugar and almond kernels, the cakes being covered with almond paste and filled with a thick egg jam.

Ingredients: 250 g of granulated sugar, 3 egg whites, 500 g of almond kernels, and soft-eggs sweet.

Confection:

The night before, blanch the almonds in very hot water to remove the skin. Blend the almonds very well until very thin.

Place in a pan, with the sugar and the whites, stirring very well. Cook, stirring constantly, in a bain-marie until thickened.

Then remove the preparation from the heat and set it aside until the next day. Tent small portions of the almond paste on a smooth surface, sprinkled with powdered sugar, and place 1 teaspoon of soft-eggs cream on each of them.

Close the cheeses, forming balls that envelop the filling well. Flatten them to form a cheese shape and let them dry.

After drying, wrap the sweets in cut tissue paper.

"Arrepiados de Almoster" - Almoster's Goosebumps

These delicious cakes come from a conventual recipe, created by the nuns of the Almoster Monastery. They are truly irresistible and simple to make, being one of the current icons of regional sweets in Santarém. The nuns who prepared the cookies for a party said that the nobles would get goosebumps just trying them, hence the name.

Ingredients: 250 g of brown sugar, 250 g of flaked almonds, 4 egg whites. It makes about 20 cookies.

Confection:

Beat the egg whites until stiff and add the sugar, continuing to beat on the same side until you get bubbles.

Add the almonds and mix, without beating too much. Grease a tray and spoon the dough into small piles, about 1 cm apart.

Preheat the oven to 150°C (302°F).

Halfway through cooking, about 20 minutes after placing the cookies in the oven, remove them and press each cake to make it fluffy.

Put them back in the oven and let them cook for another 25 minutes. Note, however, that the cooking time may need to be adjusted depending on the oven; remove the cookies when they are lightly toasted.

"Fios de ovos" - Egg threads

Threads of eggs, also known as "Royal eggs" or "Straw of Abrantes", are one of the oldest specialties of traditional Portuguese sweets. This conventual sweet is made all over the country, being an important part of a large number of traditional specialties.

Ingredients: 12 egg yolks, 2 egg whites, 250 ml of water, and 750 g of sugar.

Confection:

Mix the yolks with the whites with a fork without beating, and pass them through a sieve 3 times.

Bring the sugar with the water to the boil and let it boil until it reaches the stage of a weak pearl (the syrup runs in a thread, leaving a drop suspended at the end, as if it were a pearl). Remove all impurities from the sugar.

Put the eggs in the egg wire funnel and, without delay, drop the eggs into the syrup in small portions, handling the funnel in a circle and as high as possible. The threads will take on the appearance of a skein. Remove them with the help of one or two slotted spoons and place them on a sieve with the bottom facing up. Open the threads by running your hands through cold water.

At this point, you can pass the threads through a weaker sugar syrup (take a small portion of syrup and add a little water).

Tips: While preparing the egg strands, you should always spray them with cold water to prevent the syrup from increasing in density.

The sugar syrup should always keep boiling in the center of the pan.

To make it possible to separate the threads during cooking, add a little water, to which you add a few drops of egg yolks. The yolks, when boiled make bubbles that automatically separate the strands from the eggs.

"Pastéis de Belém" – Belém pastels

What is the difference between Belém Pastel and Custard Tart? Puff pastry and eggs are practically the same recipe. But the name "Pastel of Belém" was registered only in the pastry shop of Belém, in Lisbon, where for 100 years the original recipe exists and only there could the name be used. Belém pastels are so called because they are the specialty of an old pastry shop in this area of Lisbon, "Confeitaria de Belém, Lda". This house was founded in 1837 on the outskirts of the Jerónimos Monastery (Order of the Friars of Saint Jerome), which, legend has it, already made these cakes.

In other regions of the country, the pastries are known as "Pastel de Nata". Some argue that they are slightly different sweets because the "pastel de nata" includes the zest of 1 lemon in the cream in addition to the eggs.

The first recipe for Belém pastel was created in 1837 by the monks of the emblematic Jerome Monastery. It still remains a secret; only in the Belém pastry shop is the recipe known. The one I present here is approximate, but it is not the original.

Ingredients: half a liter of milk, 250 g of sugar, 6 egg yolks, 70 g of bread crumbs, cinnamon to taste, puff pastry, cinnamon and powdered sugar for sprinkling.

Confection:

Butter the molds suitable for pastries and line them with the puff pastry.

Mix all the ingredients and pass them through the electric mixer/blender. Fill the molds with this preparation and take them to the oven, at a low temperature, until cooked.

Serve the pastries sprinkled with cinnamon and powdered sugar.

"Pastéis de Nata" - Custard tarts

You can call them by different names: "Cream pastels", "Custard tarts", "Egg tarts" or "Cream tarts".

Ingredients: For the puff pastry: 1 pinch of salt, 300 ml of warm water, 400 g of margarine for puff pastry, 500 g of flour.
For the filling: 100 ml of water, 2 tablespoons of flour, 2 eggs, 300 g of sugar, 500 ml of milk, 7 yolks, zest of 1 lemon.

Confection:

For the puff pastry, knead the flour with the water and salt. Make a ball and make two strokes in the form of a cross to the center. Place the margarine on a piece of parchment paper and hit it with the rolling pin to get the same consistency as the dough.

Then divide the dough, pulling out the four parts it was divided into (it will form a kind of four-pointed star). Put the margarine in the center and wrap it completely with the ends. Turn the dough upside down, placing the ends on the work surface and, with a rolling pin, roll it out until you get a rectangle measuring about 40×15 cm.

Start by folding the dough into three equal parts. Turn it over and stretch it again until you have an elongated rectangle. Repeat the process of leafing the dough (folding and stretching) two more times and keep it in the fridge for 10 minutes.

After the rest, remove the dough from the refrigerator and fold it in half, bringing the ends together in the center Stretch the dough once more until it is about 4 mm thick, then sprinkle it with water along its entire length.

Roll it up evenly, cut it into slices about 1 cm thick and place each piece in a pastry tin. Allow it to rest for 10 minutes, covered.

Then dip your thumb in water, press the center of the circle and pull the dough to the top of the mold.

PS: You can alternatively buy pre-prepared dough.

For the filling:

For the filling, bring the milk to a boil with the lemon zest. Remove some of the milk and crumble the flour into it. Whisk the yolks and eggs without foaming. Remove the lemon zest and add the boiled milk, stirring well so the eggs don't cook. Then add the dissolved flour, and set aside.

Bring the sugar and water to a boil until you get a pearl stage syrup (dipping a spoon in the syrup, a ball is formed at the end of the string that runs from the spoon). Add the syrup to the milk mixture, stir and pour it into the molds, taking care not to fill them too much so that the filling does not come out during cooking.

Bake for about 25 minutes in a hot oven (250º C, 482 °F).

Unmold the custard tarts as soon as they come out of the oven.

Curiosity:

Cream pastels/ custard tart, is one of the most exported and internationally famous. In London, in some of the most famous patisseries, it can reach 3 pounds each.

The Portuguese government also helped with publicity, sponsored the "Pastel de Nata Festival" in London in 2018 and finances local businesses.

Mabílio Albuquerque, an entrepreneur from Porto, created the start-up "Nata Pura" (pure cream) and exports it internationally. From Asia to Europe, to Latin America, and eventually to the USA.

Other companies export custard tarts, but "Nata Pura" does it efficiently, selling 500,000 pastries a month in its 5000 stores around the world.

"Bolo real" - Royal cake

This cake is a typical Alentejo recipe. Almonds and gourd jam are common ingredients in Alentejo sweets and, as a convent sweet, they have eggs in abundance. The accentuated flavors of almond and gourd jam make this cake a real delight.

Ingredients: 125 g of gourd jam, 250 g of sugar + 1 spoon to add to the whites, 250 g of almond kernels, 3 egg whites, 6 yolks, powdered sugar for sprinkling.

Confection:

Grease a round shape and sprinkle it with flour. Book aside. Beat the yolks with the sugar until you get a fluffy and whitish cream. Mix the almond kernels and the gourd jam.

Beat the egg whites until stiff and, when they are almost set, add 1 tablespoon of sugar to make them firmer.

Gently mix the two preparations.

Pour into the mold and bake for 45 minutes at 160 degrees Celsius (320 degrees Fahrenheit). Don't let it dry out too much, as the royal cake should be moist.

Remove and sprinkle with powdered sugar.

"Fatias reais" - Royal Slices

Also known as "egg slices". These slices are a great way to use up leftover bread. You can eat them any time of year, but they are especially popular around Christmas.

Ingredients: 1 lemon, 12 slices of bread without crust, 12 egg yolks + 1 egg white, 250 ml of water, 750 g of sugar, and cinnamon for sprinkling.

Instructions:

Beat the yolks with the egg white. Strain the mixture through a strainer and set it aside.

Bring the sugar to the boil with the water and lemon zest. Let it boil until you get the pearl stage (when you run a thick thread of syrup, with a drop at the end).

Add a little lemon juice. Remove about half of the syrup and set aside.

Pass the slices through the yolks, letting them soak well. She drains them slightly and cooks them in the syrup on both sides. As you cook the slices, add the syrup you reserved earlier, as needed.

Place on platter and sprinkle with cinnamon.

"Migas doces" – Sweet migas

This traditional Alentejo sweet, of conventual origin, is made with bread, sugar, eggs, and cinnamon. They are part of the Christmas traditions in Alentejo, being one of the icons of regional sweets. In Portugal, "migas" is a typical dish made of bread that has been softened and then cooked, a kind of bread pudding. Here it was adapted for candy.

Ingredients: 100 g of crumbled crusty bread, 250 g of granulated sugar, 6 egg yolks, water (at taste), and cinnamon for sprinkling.

Confection:

Bring the sugar to the boil with enough water to cover it. When it boils, add the bread and stir to break it up evenly. Continue to stir until it thickens.

Remove the sweet from the heat, let it cool, and incorporate the yolks, well beaten.

Put it over low heat just to cook the yolks, stirring constantly.

Pour the sweet "migas" on plates and sprinkle with cinnamon.

Sericaia

The name cannot be translated; there is no translation. In latin, a sericaria was a woman who kept and cared for silk tissues. Perhaps the name is an allusion to the texture and lightness of the sweet. Alentejo (south region of Portugal) sweet very well-known and appreciated. Practically all Alentejo restaurants do this. The touch of cinnamon and the fluffy texture make this candy a real delight. However, the secret of the recipe, more than the ingredients, is in the way of pouring the candy on the plate, with uneven spoonfuls. This recipe was implemented in Alentejo by the skilled hands of the nuns of the convent of Elvas and Vila Viçosa.

Ingredients: 1 lemon, 1 liter of milk, 12 eggs, 150 g of wheat flour, 500 g of sugar, 1 cinnamon stick, 1 pinch of salt, and ground cinnamon.

Confection:

Bring the milk to a boil with the lemon peel, cinnamon stick, and salt. When done, remove from heat and set aside to cool. Meanwhile, beat the yolks with the sugar very well until you get a fluffy cream.

Separately, slowly dissolve the flour in the milk, then add the cream of yolks and sugar and bring to a low boil, stirring constantly.

Remove from the heat, discarding the lemon peel and cinnamon stick, and set aside to cool.

Beat the egg whites until they are stiff, and then add them carefully to the other ingredients, which should be cold or lukewarm.

In a preheated oven at 225 °C (437 °F), heat a large and deep earthenware dish.

Pour the cream onto the plate in staggered spoonfuls — one from the center to the edges of the plate and the other across.

Sprinkle generously with cinnamon and bake for 1 hour. Check, however, the doneness by doing the toothpick test — if it comes out dry, placing it in the center of the candy, the "sericaia" is ready.

Note:

When cooking the sericaia, it should have open cracks on the surface, giving it its characteristic appearance.

It is usually garnished with 1 or 2 caramelized plums, cooked in a syrup of water and sugar until caramelized.

"Bolo príncipe" - Prince cake

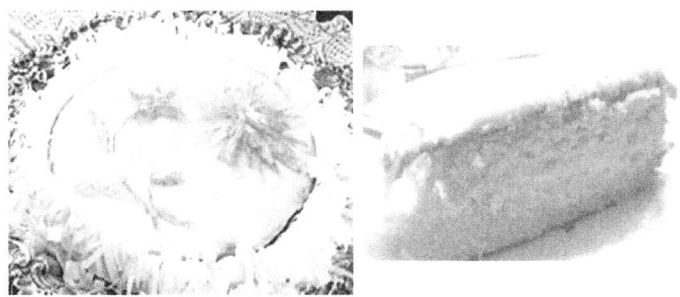

The city of Beja and other Alentejo towns were home, over the centuries, to several convents that left in the region a rich legacy of convent sweets. The Prince Cake is one of the best exponents of Alentejo convent sweets.

The ingredients used in the recipe reveal the conventual origin of this cake, which is a delight for the eyes and the palate.

Ingredients: For the cake: 1 bowl of gourd jam, 1 bowl of egg threads, 12 egg yolks, 12 bundles of eggs, 2 tablespoons of flour, 200 ml of water, 500 g of almonds, 750 g of sugar, fondant for topping (it is a paste of molten sugar that solidifies after being applied).
For decoration: covered pumpkin or candied orange peel (optional), or silver sprinkles.

Confection:

Blanch, skin and grate the almonds.

Bring the sugar to the boil with the water and let it boil until it forms a paste (when the syrup adheres to the spoon without running). Add the almonds, the well-beaten yolks, and the flour and bring everything to a boil to dry. Remove from the heat and set aside to cool.

Meanwhile, grease a tray very well and sprinkle it with flour.

Make a strip of baking parchment paper and secure the ends with pins in order to obtain a ring the size of the cake you want to make.

Take a little of the almond mass and, with your hands sprinkled with flour, flatten it, giving it the shape of a slice. Place the dough on the board, surrounding it with the strip of parchment paper.

Spread a layer of egg strands, another layer of gourd jam, and another layer of well-flattened and drained bundles on top. Cover everything with a layer of sweet almond.

Remove the paper strip, coat the entire cake with plenty of flour and put it back in to prevent the cake from spreading during cooking, which must be at a very low-temperature oven.

Once baked, remove all the flour and cover the cake with fondant. Garnish with silver sprinkles, or with strips of covered pumpkin, or candied orange.

Portalegre egg candies

The origin of this convent sweet dates back to the 18th century, when the nuns were looking for a use for the yolks. The wise mixture of eggs and sugar, combined with the time and dedication given to the recipe, results in wonderful sweets. They are traditionally wrapped in tissue paper.

Ingredients: For the candies: 200 g of sugar, 80 ml of water, 8 egg yolks, and sweet almond oil for shaping.
For the glaze: 150 ml of water, 1 tablespoon of lemon juice, and 500 g of sugar.

Confection:

Bring the sugar and water to a boil until the syrup is at a high point (shortly after it starts to boil).

Let it cool down a bit and, off the heat, add the slightly beaten egg yolks. Mix quickly so the yolks don't get curdled.

Bring the candy to the boil, stirring constantly until it forms a thick mixture. Place on a smooth and cold surface, greased with sweet almond oil, and, with also greased hands, mold the candies.

For the glaze, bring the sugar dissolved in the water and the lemon juice to a boil. Let it boil until you get a paste-like syrup (also called a weak syrup, as it is reached as soon as a small layer of sugar starts to adhere to the spoon).

Remove them immediately and, with the help of a fork or tweezers, pass the candies, one by one, through the syrup. Let them cool on the surface where you molded them and then wrap them in paper.

Saint Claire Alfitetes

The alfitetes are delicious pastries filled with almonds and grains. They are a specialty of the Saint Claire of Évora Convent. Alfitete is a culinary composition of eggs, sugar, wine, and butter.

Ingredients: 1 tablespoon of butter; 450 g of chickpeas; 450 g of blanched almonds; 675 g of sugar; 6 egg yolks; powdered sugar for sprinkling; ground cinnamon, and lard.

Confection:

The night before, soak the beans. The next day, peel it before cooking.

Once cooked, pass the beans through a grater and pour the crumbled dough into a bowl. Then grate the almonds and add them to the beans.

Bring the sugar to a boil with a small amount of water. When it is at the stage of paste, not too high, pour in the well-mixed dough, the butter, and a little cinnamon powder.

Let it boil and remove it from the heat. Then add the well-beaten yolks, stirring so that everything is evenly involved.

Bring the mixture back to the heat to bring it to a boil and, if you see that the dough is not very consistent, add a few spoonfuls of breadcrumbs, gradually (be careful not to let it get too thick, because when it cools it becomes solid). Allow to cool after removing from the heat.

Knead with a portion of the fine flour and then make the pastries.

Roll out some dough with a rolling pin, making it as thin as possible. Place spoons of stuffing on top, fold the dough in half, making the pastries and then cutting them with a reel.

Fry the cakes in lard, so they can rise, and sprinkle them with fine white sugar.

Paradise cake

This cake is a specialty of the Our Lady of Paradise Convent, in Évora. Although there are some variants of the recipe, it appears in the convent records.

Ingredients: 125 g breadcrumbs, 1350 g sugar, 15 egg yolks, 450 g ground almonds, 5 egg whites, cinnamon (as much as you need), icing or powdered sugar for topping.

Confection:

Prepare the thread-like sugar (when dipping the spoon into the syrup, the thin and crispy threads run out of it), let it cool a little, and add the grated almonds.

Bring the mixture to a boil until it thickens.

After cooling, add the yolks. Whisk everything together very well and bring it to a boil again until it thickens and makes a small castle (soft peaks).

Remove it from the heat again and stir in the breadcrumbs and cinnamon.

Finally, gently fold in the egg whites (soft peaks) without beating.

Grease a mold well with butter and pour the mixture into it. Bake in a moderate-temperature oven.

Once cool, cover the cake with sugar icing or, if you prefer, sprinkle with powdered sugar.

Drenched from the Saint Claire Convent

This is one of the most representative sweets of the rich regional sweets of Alentejo. "Encharcada" (drenched) recipes vary between the convents of Évora, Beja, and Mourão, with Évora being the most common of them all. Made from eggs, sugar, and cinnamon.

Ingredients: 200 ml of water, 22 egg yolks, 4 egg whites, 750 g of sugar, and cinnamon.

Confection:

Bring the sugar to the boil with the water and let it boil until it becomes a very weak pearl stage (when the syrup is thick, leaving a drop suspended at the limit).

Meanwhile, beat the eggs. When the syrup is ready, slowly add the eggs through a mesh strainer in circular motions. Let it cook, spearing the syrup with a spatula from the sides to the middle, to prevent it from acquiring a crust.

Remove from the heat when the eggs are cooked but still with a little syrup.

Place in a deep dish, sprinkle with cinnamon, and toast in a very hot oven for a few minutes.

"Pão de Rala" – Rala bread

This dessert, typical of Évora, integrates the very rich conventual sweets of the Alentejo. "Pão de rala" was created and made by conventual friars and nuns that existed throughout the Alentejo (south region of Portugal), and different variations are currently known from region to region. The name and appearance of the cake derive from a story, according to which King D. Sebastian visited the Convent of St. Helena of the Mount Calvary in Évora. Being a poor convent, they could only offer him "thin bread" olives and water.

Ingredients: For the dough: 300 ml of water, 500 g. of sugar, 480 g of peeled ground almonds, and 6 eggs.
For the filling: 12 egg yolks, 390 g of gourd jam, 400 g of sugar, 400 ml of water, and 6 eggs.
For the topping: powdered sugar, and egg threads (optional).

Confection:

Start by preparing the cake batter by bringing the sugar and water to the boil until it forms a paste (101° C or 213 °F, the syrup starts to bubble around the edges of the pan).

Add the grated almonds and the beaten eggs, until you get a thick mixture, then bring it to a boil over moderate heat. Stir well until the mixture comes off the pan. Remove from the heat and set aside to cool slightly.

Line a pre-greased round shape with the dough. Start by covering the bottom, pressing down well with your hands. Then line the sides with the remaining dough, well stretched and set aside.

For the filling, bring the sugar and water to a boil until you reach the thread point (105 °C or 221 °F. Dip a spoon in the syrup; it should run easily, in thread, but a thin layer of sugar should stick to the spoon).

Add 6 egg yolks to the spoonfuls, turning them over as they cook. Once ready, remove them from the heat.

Separately, mix the 6 remaining yolks with the gourd jam and let them cook.

Place the gourd jam on the previously shaped dough and arrange the two jams in alternating layers: first the gourd jam and then the layers formed with the yolks and sugar syrup. Finally, cover the filling with almond paste to give the cake the shape of a bread.

Bake for 10 to 15 minutes in a moderate oven, between 180 °C and 190 °C (374 °F). The cake should be lightly toasted, as with the bread.

Unmold only after cooling. Sprinkle with powdered sugar and decorate with egg strands, if desired.

"Torrão Real"- Royal cob

Not easy to translate, "torrão" is a kind of cake. This convent sweet, also known as "Torrão Real de Ovos" or "Torrão Doce" is one of the *ex-libris* of regional sweets in Évora. In terms of taste, it's divine.

Ingredients: 125 g of peeled ground almonds, 15 yolks, 150 ml of cream, 250 ml of water, 500 g of sugar, and ground cinnamon.

Confection:

Bring the sugar and water to the boil, letting it boil until it reaches the point of a spade (about 3 minutes, when, when dipping a spoon in the syrup, it forms a kind of blade when falling).

Remove the syrup from the heat and, when it is warm, mix the ground almonds, the beaten yolks, and the cream. Beat well to combine the ingredients well.

Bring to a boil again, over low heat, and stir until the yolks are cooked. Remove from the heat when the mixture reaches the boiling point (when you pass the spoon, you can see the bottom of the pan).

Pour the jam into a deep bowl or individual bowls. Sprinkle with cinnamon to taste.

"Filhós enroladas" - Rolled donuts

These aren't the typical donuts, but the name "filhós" didn't have an accurate translation. It is a kind of rolled up sweet dough. This recipe is traditional from Vila Viçosa, in Évora, and is one of the many traditional Christmas sweets in Alentejo. They are made from eggs and have a touch of Brandy that gives them a distinct flavor. The sugar syrup makes them a real gift from heaven. They stand out from traditional donuts for their shape, crunchy texture, and flavor.

Ingredients: For the dough: 1 tablespoon of sugar, 1 tablespoon of lard, 1 tablespoon of butter, 100 ml of Brandy, 6 eggs, flour (as needed). **For the syrup:** 1 kg of sugar.

Confection:

Beat the eggs very well with the lard, butter, brandy and a spoon of sugar.

Add the flour and knead until you get an elastic dough that stretches well. Let it rest a little.

Meanwhile, put the oil on the fire.

Roll out the dough and cut strips of about 7 x 20 cm. Take one end in your hand and hold the other end with a long fork. Insert the fork with the tip of the dough into the boiling oil and roll it up while letting it fall.

Let the donuts fry until they are golden and then roll them in sugar at the stage of flying (when you remove a little syrup with a skimmer and blow, balls are formed that come off like soap bubbles).

Almond Cake from the Vidigueira Convent

The recipe was created by the nuns of the Vidigueira Convent to mark the day of Saint Rita of Cascia, celebrated on May 22. For this reason, this almond cake is also known as "Saint Rita of Cascia Cake". It is made from almonds and sprinkled with powdered sugar, and can also be decorated with skinless almonds.

Ingredients: 1 small spoon of cinnamon, 500 g of sugar, 500 g of blanched almonds, 100 g of wheat flour, 6 whole eggs and 6 yolks, powdered sugar (for sprinkling), and flaked skinless almonds (for decoration).

Confection:

Grate the almonds. In a bowl, beat the sugar, almonds, eggs, and yolks very well. Add the cinnamon and beat some more. Then add the flour and mix well, without beating.

Let the dough rest for about half an hour. Then place it in a greased and floured shape and bake it in a hot oven for about 15 minutes.

After it has cooled, take it out of the mold and sprinkle it with powdered sugar. If you want, you can decorate it with skinless almonds.

Conceição Convent Sweets

This secular sweet became known by the name of the Convent where it was created - the old Convent of Conceição, currently being the headquarters of the Regional Museum of Beja. It is one of the traditional sweets of Alentejo.

Ingredients: 1 teaspoon of butter, 18 egg yolks, 2 egg whites, 500 g of sugar, and 250 ml of water.

Confection:

Put the sugar on the fire with the water and let it boil until the pearl point (108° C or 226 °F, when the sugar syrup is allowed to drain on the spoon and at the end a small pearl of syrup forms).

Remove from the heat and set aside to cool. Add the yolks and whites, previously mixed, and the butter. Pour the mixture into small round shapes but with a rounded bottom, and bake in a moderate-temperature oven.

Place in crimped paper boxes after unmolding while still hot.

"Queijadas de Requeijão" - Cheesecakes Tarts

Pastels and "Queijadas" in English can be translated as tarts, these ones are made with cheese curd, lard and eggs. Beja's cheese tarts delight everyone who tastes them. Its sweet filling is contained in dough shapes that complete the enveloping sweetness.

Ingredients:
For the dough: half a tablespoon of lard, half a tablespoon of butter, 1 egg, 1 pinch of salt, 50 ml of warm water, and 125 g of flour.
For the filling: 1 teaspoon of cinnamon, 2 tablespoons of flour, 3 eggs and 3 egg yolks, 375 g of sugar, 50 g of butter, and 500 g of cheese curd.

Confection:

Prepare the dough, working the ingredients and kneading them with the warm water seasoned with salt. Knead the dough very well and let it rest.

Meanwhile, prepare the filling. Pass the cheese curd through the sieve and, stirring very well, add the remaining ingredients. With the kitchen roll pin, roll out the dough on a smooth surface, leaving a very thin layer.

Cut slices about 8 cm in diameter and, with them, line muffin tins, greased and sprinkled.

Fill the molds with the curd filling and bake in a moderate-temperature oven.

Pumpkin and Carrot tarts

Ingredients: 200 g of pumpkin, 400 g of carrots, 250 g of sugar, 1 cinnamon stick, 1 teaspoon of cinnamon powder, zest of 1 orange, 50 g of self-rising flour, 4 eggs, butter for greasing, and 1 natural yogurt.

Preparation:

Start the recipe by peeling the pumpkin and carrots and cooking them in water seasoned with salt and a cinnamon stick. When they are tender, they are already cooked.

Then, drain the pumpkin and carrots and grind them very well with the help of the electric mixer/blender, until you get a puree.

Meanwhile, turn on the oven to a temperature of 180° C (356 °F).

In a large bowl, place the puree obtained and add the sugar, cinnamon powder, and orange zest. Combine everything thoroughly.

Then, add the eggs, one by one, and mix everything very well.

It's time to add the flour and natural yogurt and beat some more.

Now, grease the molds with butter and put the mixture in them.

Place the pumpkin and carrot tarts in the oven for approximately 20 minutes.

Wafer cheeses

This is the name by which delicious cakes of convent origin are currently known, with almonds and lots of eggs, which influenced the regional sweets of Beja and Alentejo in general. However, the original name of these sweets was "Queijadinhas de Hostia" (wafer tarts).

The base and top are formed by slices of wafers. In the center, they are filled with egg jam that gives them a delicious yellow hue. There are variants, some higher than others, with a thinner or thicker wafer layer (to taste). "Hóstia" is the edible paper, it has many names, "host", "wafer", but you can use edible rice paper.

Ingredients: 18 egg yolks, 2 egg whites, 200 ml of water, 250 g of peeled and ground almonds, 500 g of sugar, soft eggs for the filling, and wafer slices.

Preparation:
Mix the yolks with the egg whites. Bring the sugar and water to the boil, letting it boil until it forms a strong paste. Add the almonds to the sugar syrup. Remove for a moment from the heat and add the beaten eggs.

Allow to thicken on low heat until you can see the bottom of the pan. Let cool completely.

Take slices of wafers (you can buy already made wafers for sweets).

When the almond paste is very cold, mold it into some rolls that you will place between the slices of wafer, forming rings. Fill the dough rings with soft-eggs cream and top with another wafer slice.

Gourd jam Cake with Almonds

Sweet from the Algarve (south of Portugal), much appreciated at Easter and Christmas.

Ingredients:
For the dough: 100 g of ground almonds, 100 g of flour, 150 g of gourd jam threads, 250 g of sugar, 250 g of butter, and 6 eggs.
For the topping: powdered sugar, toasted flaked almonds.

Confection:
Cream together the butter and sugar until smooth.

Mix the yolks, the gourd jam, the almonds, the flour, and, finally, the beaten egg whites. Grease and sprinkle a round shape and take it to the oven, previously heated to 200° C (392 °F), for 45 minutes.

When serving, sprinkle with powdered sugar and toasted almonds.

Algarvian marzipan and almond cookies

These candies are also a work of art. In various shapes and then hand-painted with food coloring, they are beautiful.

In the Algarve, they are sold to tourists and locals in all the bakeries.

Ingredients: 500 g of almond kernels, 500 g of sugar, 1 egg white, food coloring of different colors, 1 small brush, and egg jam or gourd jam for filling.

Confection:

Blanch the almonds, drain, and peel. Grind them until they are powdered.

In a large bowl, mix the almonds, now powdered, with the sugar. Add the egg white and, using your hands, slowly knead to incorporate everything.

At this point, the dough can be shaped next, or it can rest for an hour or two or even from one day to the next.

Shape the almond paste into different shapes (puppies, stars, etc.), and fill them.

Color with food coloring, using a small brush with gentle movements.

Place them in small paper cups.

"Bolo delícia" - Delight cake

This typical Algarve cake is made with traditional ingredients from the region, such as almonds and gourd jam. It is also called "Three Delights Cake" (and has 3 layers). As a recipe from Portuguese cuisine, it maintains one of the characteristics of this confectionery, which is that the dough is prepared with a large amount of egg yolks. Cinnamon is another of the reference ingredients to be used in this recipe.

Ingredients: half a kilo of sugar, 30 egg yolks, 200 g of gourd jam, 300 g of almonds, 5 g of cinnamon, 50 g of pumpkin in syrup, 70 g of margarine butter.

Preparation:

Bring the sugar to the boil until it reaches the point of strong threads (after the sugar has been boiling for some time, it forms a strong thread between your fingers without breaking).

Pour the sugar syrup over the yolks, stirring quickly. Add the almonds, margarine, and pumpkin to the slivers. Bring it to a boil to thicken.

Grease a loaf pan with butter and baking paper, and layer the dough with cinnamon and butter in between each layer.

Put it on the fire to dry a little. Remove it and decorate to your liking.

Dom Rodrigos

Also known as "Dom Rodrigo cookies", these traditional sweets, originating in Lagos, are one of the most typical sweets from the Algarve region. They are made of egg threads that have been spiced up with cinnamon and almonds, which are common in sweets from the Algarve region.

Ingredients: for six servings: 50 ml of water, 250 g of sugar, 250 g of egg threads, 4 egg yolks, 50 g of ground almonds, and ground cinnamon.

Confection:

Bring to the boil 200 grams of sugar covered in water and let it form a pearl point.

Remove it from the heat and stir in the almonds. Let it cool down, add the yolks and put it back on the heat, stirring until it thickens. Sprinkle with a little ground cinnamon.

With the remaining sugar and water, make a syrup in threads point (103° C or 217 °F).

Place the syrup in a skillet and bring it to a boil. When it boils, pour the egg threads and, over them, the mixture made with sugar, almonds, and yolks.

With the help of two spatulas, wrap the egg strands around the filling, enveloping it completely. Let it brown and remove it from the skillet.

Cut six squares of crystal paper and as many squares of colored silver paper with a slightly larger dimension. Separate the preparation into equal amounts by the squares, join the ends of each one and roll them up, forming a rough pyramid.

Once cold, Dom Rodrigos are ready to be savored.

Almond Cheeses

The almond cheeses are the result of the combination of almonds with sugar and eggs, and one of the wonders of Algarve sweets is used in their confection: the soft-eggs sweet.

Ingredients: 1 cup of soft-eggs cream, 1 egg white, 250 g of sugar, 250 g of blanched almonds, powdered sugar (for the topping).

Confection:

You must grind the almonds very well to get a powder. Add them to the sugar, mix well and knead as you add the white. Work the repair until you get a well-bonded thin mass.

Put it on the fire to dry and let it rest for a few hours.

After the rest period, divide the dough into balls about the size of small cheese. Cut about 1/4 of the portion from each to make a lid. Shape what's left of the ball, giving it the shape of a small cheese.

Fill the balls with soft-eggs and close them with the lid of almond paste, smoothing well with a wet knife.

Mold again with powdered sugar until you get a cake with the shape of a cheese. Then dust the surface with powdered sugar and serve.

Madeiran tarts

The sweets of Madeira Island are very rich in the combination of flavors and traditions of the archipelago, namely with regard to the ingredients used. These tarts are one of the most popular regional sweets in Madeira. Made with curd cheese, eggs, and sugar, these convent sweets are delicious.

Ingredients:
For the dough: for 20 tarts, 2 tablespoons of sugar, 250 g of wheat flour, 250 g of butter.
For the filling: 1 egg white, 1 (small) spoon of cinnamon, 250 g of sugar, 250 g of curd cheese, 6 egg yolks, butter or jam (for greasing).

Confection:

Sift the flour with the sugar. Add the butter and work the ingredients to obtain a well-bound dough. Let the dough rest for 4 or 5 hours.

Meanwhile, pass the cheese through a fine sieve. Add the sugar and mix well. If you want to soften the flavor of the curd, add the lemon zest and cinnamon.

Add the yolks individually, mixing well between each addition, and the egg white.

Whisk everything until a homogeneous mixture is obtained.

After the dough rests, roll it out to be very thin and cut it into squares. In the center of each square, place a spoonful of the filling. Fold the ends over this one so that the center is visible.

Place the tarts on a tray on top of squares of baking parchment paper.

Bake for about 15 minutes in a very hot oven (220° C, 428 °F).

When they come out of the oven, grease the tarts while they are still hot with butter or jam.

Cornucopias - Cornucopies

Cornucopies are a specialty of Angra do Heroísmo, a city on the island of Terceira. Regarding their origin, it is known that they were created by the wise and experienced hands of the nuns, being one of the countless relics of Portuguese conventual sweets. The appearance of the "cornucópia" resembles that of a sea whelk.

Ingredients:
For the dough: 2 teaspoons of butter, 2 tablespoons of lard, 2 tablespoons of sugar, 2 tablespoons of toasted and grated bread, 4 tablespoons of ground almonds, 500 g of flour.
For the filling: 12 egg yolks, 500 g of sugar.
To brush: 2 egg whites.

Confection:

Grease the "cornucopie moulds" very well and set them aside. Combine the ingredients indicated for the dough with very hot water, added as it is being absorbed. Knead very well and let it rest. Roll out the dough thin, cutting a strip into triangles.

Involve the shapes in these triangles of dough, pass through the beaten egg white and then through the almonds mixed with the breadcrumbs. Bake in a very hot oven.

Unmold carefully, almost cold. Fill with soft-eggs and a sweet made with the ingredients listed above.

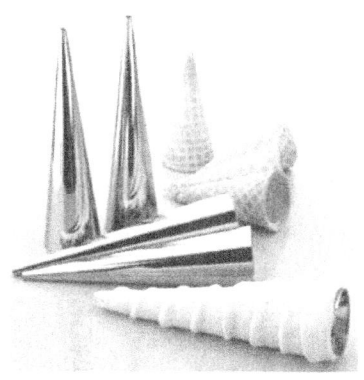

Moulds

Vila Franca do Campo tarts

The recipe for these tarts was created by the nuns of the former Saint Andreas Convent, in Vila Franca do Campo, on the island of São Miguel, Azores. They are, therefore, one of the relics of Azorean convent sweets, being much appreciated and the most sought-after regional sweets on the island.

Ingredients:
For the dough: 1 tablespoon (small) sugar, 1 tablespoon (soup spoon) butter, 1 tablespoon (soup spoon) of lard, 1 egg, 250 g of flour, salt (as needed).
For the filling and topping: 1 egg white, 1 teaspoon of butter, 1

tablespoon of flour, 2 liters of milk, 250 g of sugar, 6 egg yolks, powdered sugar, and cheese rennet.

Confection:

Start by preparing the filling. Warm the milk, adding the cheese rennet in the proportions indicated. Cover the container and let it curdle.

Remove the rennet with a cloth and squeeze out the whey in order to obtain a very dry mass. Knead until very thin.

Add the yolks, egg white, sugar, butter, and flour. Bring to a low boil after thoroughly mixing. Remove from heat and, once cool enough to handle, strain through a sieve or fine strainer. Reserve it for the fridge.

The dough should be prepared the next day.

Knead the indicated ingredients with a little warm water in order to obtain a dough that you can stretch. Wrap it in a napkin and let it rest.

With the rolling pin and sprinkle of flour roll out the thin dough. With a glass or a pastry cutter, cut it into circles with a diameter of 12 cm. As you cut them, let them air out on the table.

Then, in the center of each circle, place a mound of the prepared filling. Adjusting it with a toothpick, pull the dough up, touching it to the filling and making a fluted box.

Around each tart, place a strip of parchment paper about 2 cm high, which will support the dough (the paper is fastened with a pin).

Bake the tarts in a medium temperature oven and, once cooked, sprinkle the surface abundantly with powdered sugar.

Jesuits

The Jesuits are pastries made of puff pastry and sugar and sold throughout the national territory. However, the traditional and true Jesuits are the ones from Santo Tirso. It is believed that the recipe arrived in Portugal through the hands of a Spanish pastry chef who worked, at the time, at the Moura confectionery in Santo Tirso. He had previously worked in a community of Jesuit priests in Bilbao.

Ingredients: 460 g of puff pastry, **For the filling:** 250 ml semi-skimmed milk, 1 egg and 2 egg yolks, 40 g of flour, 75 g of sugar. **For the topping:** 2 egg whites, 6 tablespoons of sugar (soup spoon).

Confection:

Preheat the oven to 200° C (392 °F). Boil 200 ml of milk. In a bowl, mix the egg, yolks, flour and sugar with the remaining cold milk (50 ml). Add this mixture to the hot milk, still on the heat, stirring constantly until you get a thick cream.

Remove from the heat and set aside to cool, stirring frequently.

Roll out the puff pastry and cut into strips about 4 mm thick. Spread the strips with the cream, place another strip of puff pastry on top and cut them into triangles.

Place the triangles of dough on an oven tray lined with parchment paper.

For the topping, beat the egg whites and gradually add the sugar, beating until you get a thin meringue. Spread the top of the triangles with this mixture and put them in the oven until they are cooked to your liking.

Note: Some people like to add a few strands of gourd jam to the filling.

"Travesseiros de Sintra" – Pillows of Sintra

Delicious puff pastries filled with egg and almond cream. They appeared at the "Confeitaria Piriquita", in the 40's, when the founder's daughter, Mrs. Constância, developed the recipe.

Ingredients: 800 g of puff pastry (2 leaves), 600 g of sugar, 300 g of ground almonds, 8 egg yolks, 2 dl water, 1 small spoon of ground cinnamon, flour for dusting, and powdered sugar (for dusting).

Confection:

Bring the water and sugar to the boil in a pan and let it boil for 8 minutes. Mix in the ground almonds, then remove from the heat and set aside to cool slightly. Stir the yolks slightly, add them to the pan, mix well and bring to a boil, stirring constantly until it boils. Remove it from the heat, add the cinnamon, mix well and let it cool.

Preheat the oven to 180°C (356°F). Spread the puff pastry with the rolling pin on the table sprinkled with flour, leaving it with a thin thickness and in the shape of a rectangle. Then cut it into small rectangles about 15 x 6 cm. Pour some of the almond mixture on top of each rectangle, then fold over to make "pillows" and close the ends tightly.

Place them on the oven tray previously rinsed with cold water and bake them in the oven for about 20 minutes, or until golden brown. Allow to cool before serving sprinkled with powdered sugar.

Sintra cheese tarts

Much older recipe. "Queijada" is a pastry made with eggs, cheese, flour, and cinnamon, which was even mentioned by Eça de Queiroz in one of his works. Its origin comes from the medieval period, when the city had a large cheese production. In documents from the 13th and 14th centuries, there are records that refer to "Queijadas" tarts as a form of payment, at least since 1227. The earliest records are from 1756, when Maria Sapa produced the first queijadas in Ranholas (Sintra).

Ingredients:

For dough: 250 g of flour, 50 g of butter margarine, 1 egg, flour (for dusting).
For the filling: 4 small fresh cheeses, 6 egg yolks, 250 g of sugar, 1 tablespoon of flour, 1 dl of water, ground cinnamon, and powdered sugar.

Confection:

Mix all the above ingredients for the dough and knead them well. Roll out the dough on a flour-dusted countertop until it is very thin. Cut into circles, line small shapes and trim the edges. Book aside.

Prepare the filling: bring the water and sugar to the boil in a pan until it becomes pearly. Beat the yolks well with the flour and then add the previous mixture in a stream, beating constantly. Pass the cheeses through a fine mesh strainer and wrap them with the dough. Mix in some cinnamon and stir.

Distribute the mixture into the molds and bake for 35 minutes at 180 o C (356 °F). Allow to cool before unmolding and serving sprinkled with powdered sugar.

Custard pie with condensed milk

Identical to the custard tart (Pastel de Nata).

Ingredients: 1 rolled puff pastry roll, 1 can of condensed milk, 8 eggs, 200 ml of cream, and lemon zest (if you like).

Confection:

Unroll the puff pastry and line a metallic pie tin with it. Trim the edges and prick the bottom with a fork. Reserve.

In a bowl, pour the condensed milk, cream, and eggs and beat well. Add lemon zest to taste (if you like) and beat some more.

Fill the pie tin with the previous preparation and take it to the oven, preheated to 200° C (392 °F), until the pie is cooked and golden. Remove from the oven, set aside to cool, and serve.

Bean tarts

Ingredients: 400 g of puff pastry, 1 can of white beans, 500 g of sugar, 12 egg yolks, 300 ml of water, 1 cinnamon stick, 1 lemon peel, and powdered sugar (as much as you need).

Confection:

Drain the beans, rinse with water, and drain again. Then pass it through the passe-vite and reserve.

Bring the water, sugar, cinnamon stick, and lemon zest to the boil in a pan and let it boil until it becomes pearly. Then stir in the bean puree and remove from the heat.

In a separate bowl, beat the yolks and gradually add the previous preparation, stirring constantly. Pour back into the pan and heat until thickened. Remove from heat and set aside.

Roll out the puff pastry in a rectangular shape, brush with water and roll into a pie shape. Cut into slices about 1 inch thick and arrange one in each shape. Wet your fingertips in water and stretch the dough around the inside of the mould until lined.

Fill the moulds lined with the bean filling, sprinkle with powdered sugar and bake in the oven, preheated to 200° C (392 °F), for 25 minutes. Remove from the oven and serve the decorated pastries to taste.

"Bolo de bolacha" - Wafer cake

Ingredients: 300 g of biscuit cookies, 300 g of butter, 150 g of powdered sugar, 2 eggs, sweetened coffee (can be a full mug), and crushed cookies.

Confection:

In a bowl, beat the butter with the powdered sugar and the eggs until you obtain a homogeneous cream. Book aside.

Dip the cookies in coffee, spread them with the cream and arrange them in layers on a plate. Cover the surface with the remaining cream and sprinkle with crushed cookies. Put it in the fridge until firm.

"Folar doce de Miranda" - Miranda's sweet bread

It is a sweet cake from Miranda do Douro with an intense cinnamon flavor. The dough, similar to that of sponge cake but thinner, is interspersed with layers of sugar and cinnamon filling. At Easter, I consider this one of the best cakes! Also known as Miranda's "Sweet Ball". In the Algarve, in Olhão, it is practically the same cake.

Ingredients: 750 g of flour, 300 g of dark brown sugar, 150 g of butter, 4 dl of milk and 2 additional spoons of milk, 3 large eggs and 1 yolk, 1 spoon of sugar, 1 sachet of dry yeast, 1 pinch of fine salt, ground cinnamon, butter for greasing, and flour for sprinkling.

Confection:

Place the flour on a benchtop, add the salt and sugar, mix well and make a small cavity. Then add the yeast dissolved in the 4 dl of warm milk, the previously beaten eggs, and the butter and beat very well until a homogeneous and well-beaten dough forms. Place in a bowl sprinkled with flour, make a cross cut, cover with a damp cloth and let it rise until it doubles in volume.

Grease a pan with butter. Knead the dough again, divide it into five layers, roll out one layer, place it on the board, and sprinkle with a little brown sugar and cinnamon powder to taste. Repeat the operation until the ingredients are used up. Cover again with a damp cloth and leave to rise for another 30 minutes.

Brush with the egg yolk previously mixed with the 2 tablespoons of milk and bake for 40 minutes at 180 °C (356 °F) or until cooked. Remove from the oven, unmold, cool, cut into cubes, and decorate as desired.

Gelatin with Condensed Milk

Gelatin with condensed milk is a fresh and very delicious dessert. Prepare this recipe in advance as you have to allow time for the jellies to solidify.

Ingredients: 1 strawberry jello, 4 jellies of different flavors, 1 pack of cream, 1 can of condensed milk.

Confection:

First, prepare the four jellies of different flavors and put them in the fridge to solidify.

When ready, cut the jellies into squares and set them aside.

Now, dissolve the strawberry gelatin in a glass of cold water and another of hot water.

In the mixer, place the condensed milk, the cream, and the dissolved strawberry gelatin. Beat everything very well for 5 minutes.

Finally, pour this mixture into a cake tin or platter, and mix in the previously reserved pieces of gelatin.

Put it back in the fridge to solidify.

Moist Orange Pie

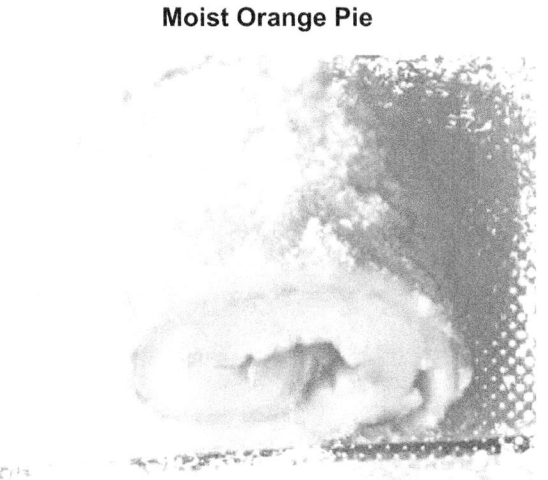

Ingredients: 250 ml of orange juice (preferably natural juice), 500 g of sugar, 50 g of flour, 8 large eggs, zest of 1 orange, margarine for greasing, sugar for sprinkling at the end.

Confection:

Grease a tray with margarine, line it with parchment paper, and grease it again. Preheat the oven to 180°C (356°F).

In a bowl, mix the sugar with the flour, add the orange juice, zest, and eggs and beat well.

Pour the dough onto the tray and bake in the oven for about 15 to 20 minutes. Remove from the oven. Unmold onto a kitchen towel sprinkled with sugar and roll up. Allow to cool before garnishing to taste.

Farófias

They are made with egg whites. The oldest recipe for a preparation identical to that of "farófias" comes from the Our Lady Conceição Convent, in Loulé, and is called "Clouds".

Ingredients: 300 g of sugar, 12 eggs, 1 cinnamon stick, 1 lemon peel, and ground cinnamon (for sprinkling).

Confection:

Separate the yolks from the whites (keep the yolks in a bowl). Beat the egg whites until stiff, adding half the sugar slowly.

Heat a large skillet with plenty of water. Bring to a boil with the cinnamon stick and lemon zest. Lower the heat, add spoonfuls of the whites, a few at a time, and cook for 20 seconds on each side. Remove the "farófias" with a slotted spoon, letting them drain, and place them in a bowl.

In a saucepan, mix the remaining sugar with 120 ml of water and the egg yolks. Bring it to a boil, stirring constantly until it thickens without letting it boil. Remove from the heat. Now pour this yolk cream over the "farófias" and serve sprinkled with ground cinnamon.

Creamy Sweet Rice

Ingredients: 300 g of medium rice or risotto, 350 g of sugar, 2 l of fat whole milk, 6 yolks, 6 dl of water, 1 tablespoon of butter, 1 lemon peel, 1 pinch of salt, 1 cinnamon stick; and ground cinnamon (for sprinkling at the end).

Confection:

To prepare this rice pudding, pour the water into a pan, add the butter, a pinch of salt, the lemon peel, and the cinnamon stick, and bring to a boil. Add the rice and cook, stirring occasionally, until it runs out of water.

In a separate pan, heat the milk. Then add the milk to the rice pan, little by little, stirring gradually, and let the rice cook until it becomes soft and creamy. Then add the sugar, stir, and let it boil for another 5 minutes.

In a bowl, beat the yolks. Add some of the rice from the pan, stirring until warm. Then add to the pan, stirring constantly. Remove from the heat, discard the lemon peel and cinnamon stick, and pour into a bowl. Let cool. When serving, sprinkle with cinnamon.

Note: To achieve a creamier texture, use whole milk in this risotto. Some people, instead of egg yolks, add Norwegian sour cream to rice.

Lemon "S" Cookies

Cookies made in the shape of an "S", in the oven with a lemon aroma.

Ingredients: 100 g of softened butter margarine, 125 g of sugar, lemon zest, 1 tablespoon of lemon juice, 350 g of wheat flour, 1 small spoon of yeast, 1 tablespoon of milk, powdered sugar for sprinkling.

Confection:

In a bowl, beat the margarine with the sugar and the lemon zest until you get a white and fluffy mass. Slowly add the beaten egg and lemon juice, beating well after each addition.

Sift the flour with the yeast and add it to the mixture. Mix well. Add the milk and mix again until you get a soft dough. Take out small pieces of dough, make rolls, and make the cookies in the desired shape.

Place the cookies on greased and floured trays and bake in the oven, preheated to 160° C (320 °F), for 15 – 20 minutes. After this time, remove them and transfer them to a cake cooling rack.

Lastly, sprinkle with powdered sugar.

Molotof pudding

Another wonderful recipe, similar to the "Farófias", is made with egg whites and yolks.

Ingredients: 12 eggs, 300 g of sugar, 100 ml of water, butter for greasing, and sugar for sprinkling.

Confection:

Grease a mold with butter and sprinkle it with sugar. Reserve. Preheat the oven to 180°C (356°F).

Beat the egg whites, gradually adding half the sugar. Pour into the tin, flatten, and bake in the oven for 12 minutes. After that time, turn off the oven and let it cool for 30 minutes to 1 hour. Then remove it and unmold.

Place the remaining sugar, water and egg yolks in a saucepan, stirring constantly until it thickens. Remove from heat, strain through a mesh strainer, and set aside to cool. Pour the cream over the Molotof and store it in the fridge. Serve fresh.

Algarvian almonds Tart

Algarve recipe.

Here's the traditional almond pie recipe made in the Algarve. Delicious and easy to prepare, this is the most popular recipe, but if you want to make a faster variation, change the base to ready-made shortcrust pastry.

Ingredients: Base: 150 g of flour, 100 g of sugar, 1 egg, 100 g of butter, 1 small spoon of yeast, 3 tablespoons of milk.

Ingredients for the filling: 150 g of sliced almonds, 100 g of sugar, 125 g of butter, 3 tablespoons of milk, and a pinch of salt.

Confection:

Start by making the base. Mix the sugar, egg and softened butter.

After the mixture is homogeneous, add the milk and the flour with the yeast and mix well without beating.

Finally, grease a pie crust with a little butter and flour, pour the dough inside and flatten it to the desired shape, place it in a preheated oven at 180 o C (356 °F) for about 15 minutes to settle and get half cooked, remove it from the oven and set it aside.

Now for the filling: in a small pan, add all the stuffing ingredients; the almond, sugar, butter, milk, and a pinch of salt, mix and heat for a few minutes until it boils; in total, about 5 or 6 minutes, just to mix the ingredients well.

Pour all the mixture over the base and return it to the oven at 356 °F until it is well caramelized on top, which should be around 15 minutes, and it's ready to serve.

Apple Stuffed Toasts

Ingredients: 300 g of apple jam, 6 small breads from the last day, 2 large eggs, 500 ml of milk, sugar-cinnamon mixture (for sprinkling), oil for frying.

Confection:

Slightly remove the crust from the breads. Open them, divide the apple candy between them, and close them again. Pass them through the warm milk and squeeze them lightly. Then pass them through the beaten eggs and fry them on both sides in hot oil. Remove from the oven and drain on absorbent paper.

After draining, roll the French toasts in a mixture of sugar and cinnamon. Serve with garnishes to taste.

Olive oil Cookies

They are a temptation!

Ingredients: 325 g of sugar, 300 g of wheat flour, 250 g of corn flour, 1 dl of olive oil, 1 dl of water, 1 orange, 1 small spoon of ground fennel, flour to taste, frying oil, and sugar for sprinkling.

Confection:

In a bowl, place the flours, sugar, and fennel and mix. Add the orange juice and zest and drizzle with the boiling oil, stirring constantly. Add the warm water and knead well.

With floured hands, make small, round buns and then fry them in hot oil. Remove, drain well, and sprinkle with sugar before serving.

"Sonhos de abóbora" - Pumpkin Dreams

They are really a dream.

Ingredients: 130 g of unleavened flour, 250 ml of water, 3 large eggs, 1 tablespoon of unsalted butter, 1 teaspoon of baking powder, frying oil, salt to taste. **For the syrup:** 350 g of sugar, 200 ml of water, 1 cinnamon stick, 1 orange peel, and 1 lemon peel.

Confection:

Prepare the syrup: bring the water, sugar, cinnamon stick, and orange and lemon rinds to the boil. Let it boil for 10 minutes, stirring occasionally. Remove it from heat and set aside.

Sift the flour with a pinch of salt. Dissolve it in 150 ml of cold water. Bring 100 ml of water to a boil and, when it starts to boil, add the butter. Add the dissolved flour and stir continuously. Remove it from the heat when the dough comes off the pan.

Let the dough cool a little, sprinkle with the yeast and mix well. Add the eggs, one at a time, mixing between each addition. Beat the dough until it starts to bubble.

Heat a pan with oil and let it heat up. Add spoonfuls of the dough and let it fry, over medium heat, until it gains color (prick with a fork, so they don't get undercooked). Remove them with a slotted spoon and let them drain on absorbent paper.

Arrange the pastries on a plate, drizzle them with the syrup and serve them at room temperature.

Yogurt and Egg Pudding

Ingredients: 2 natural yogurts, 1 can of condensed milk, 600 ml of milk, 4 large eggs, 5 tablespoons of liquid caramel (to grease the mold).

Confection:

Bring a large, wide pot of water to the fire and bring it to a boil. Grease a form of pudding with the caramel.

Place the eggs in the blender cup, add the condensed milk, the yogurts and the milk, turn it on and let it beat well. Then pour it into the mold, cover well, place it in the pan with the water on the heat and let it cook for 50 minutes (like in a bain-marie). Turn off the heat and let the pudding cool in the water.

Then take it to the fridge, unmold it and serve it very cold.

"Doce da Casa"- House dessert

This pudding is divine.

Ingredients: 100 g of biscuit cookies, 100 g of sugar, 2 cans of condensed milk, 5 dl of milk, 4 dl of cream, 6 egg yolks, 1 tablespoon of cornstarch, granulated chocolate (to decorate), and coffee (to soak the cookies).

Confection:

Pour the condensed milk into a pan, add the milk and bring to the boil, stirring constantly until it boils. Remove from the heat.

In a bowl, mix the egg yolks with the cornstarch flour, then add the milk mixture, whisking constantly. Pour back into the pan and bring to the boil, stirring continuously until it thickens. Remove from heat, divide into 6 individual bowls, and set aside to cool.

Soak the cookies in warm sugared coffee and distribute them on top. In a bowl, beat the cream into whipped cream until very firm, gradually adding the sugar and beating constantly. Place in a pastry bag, pipe on top of the cookies, and sprinkle with chocolate sprinkles to serve.

Chocolate salami

It is said that this recipe for this sweet is typical of Portugal but also of Italy.

Ingredients: 200 g of biscuit cookies, 100 g of powdered chocolate, 100 g of sugar, 100 g of melted butter, 1 beaten egg, and aluminum foil (for wrapping).

Confection:

For this chocolate salami recipe, crush the crackers and pour them into a bowl. Add the chocolate powder, sugar, melted butter, and beaten egg and mix everything very well until you get a moldable dough.

Shape the mixture into a salami shape and wrap it in aluminum foil. Place it in the fridge for a few hours, until it has a very hard consistency and can be cut without falling apart.

Serve the chocolate salami in slices, without the aluminum foil, and decorate to taste.

"Tabefe" - Slap

It is a tasty pudding from the Douro Litoral. "Tabefe" means a slap.

Ingredients: 3.5 dl of milk, 280 g of sugar, salt (as needed), and 5 egg yolks.

Instructions:

Bring the milk, salt, and sugar to a boil in a saucepan. Remove from the heat. Pour into a bowl and let it cool.

Add the yolks and stir until a homogeneous mixture is obtained. Pour into clay bowls. Preheat the oven to 250 °C (482 °F).

Let it cool.

"Linguas de Sogra" - Mother-in-law's tongues

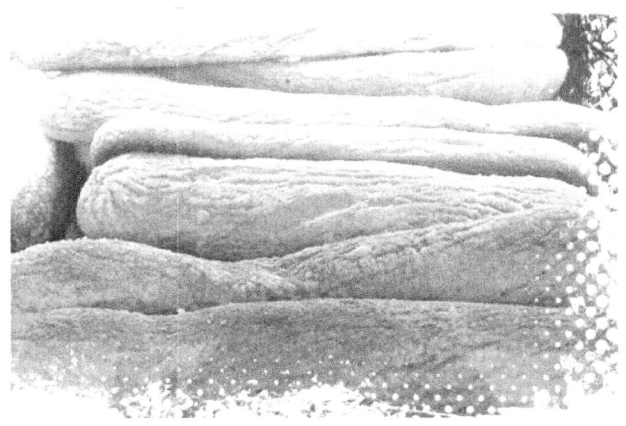

I don't know if the recipe is typical Portuguese, but I know that in my childhood I ate many, and they were on sale in all bakeries.

It's a delicious cake.

Ingredients: 500 g of wheat flour, 1 pinch of vanilla sugar, 2 units of egg yolks, 100 g of margarine, 1 pinch of salt, 2 tablespoons of powdered milk, half a glass of water, 80 g of sugar, 100 g of flour of wheat, 50 g of fresh yeast.

Topping: 2 egg yolks, water (to make a creamy point, to taste), 100 g of sugar, 100 g of grated coconut, and ground cinnamon.

Confection:
Make a paste with 100 g of wheat flour, fresh yeast and 1/2 cup of water. After fermentation, add all the other dough ingredients. After making the dough, let it rest for about 20 minutes.

Divide the dough into 8 parts, making rolls. Brush with egg and cover with the topping frosting.

Topping:
Mix the topping ingredients and use.
Wait for at least 30 minutes to rise.
Bake for 15 to 20 minutes in a preheated oven (180 °C, 356 °F).

After roasting, spread apricot jam over the top, to shine (optional).

Jams, jellies

It is tasty, to spread on bread, toast, or crackers. Fill pies, add to yogurt, etc.

Pumpkin jam

Ingredients: 1.5 kg of pumpkin, 1 kg of sugar, 2 cinnamon sticks, juice of 1 lemon, and zest of 1 orange.

Confection:

Cut the pumpkin into pieces and put them in a pan. Add the cinnamon sticks, lemon juice, orange peel, and sugar and mix.

Then put it on a low heat for about 1 hour and 45 minutes, stirring occasionally. Remove from the heat, discard the cinnamon sticks and orange peel, and puree to a smooth consistency. Return to the heat, bring to a boil, then remove from the heat, cool, and pour into glass jars with lids. Store in a cool place, protected from light, and serve it with fresh cheese, cottage cheese, etc.

Tangerine jam

Ingredients: 1 kg of tangerine segments, 600 g of sugar, 200 ml of tangerine juice. Use natural juice from the fruit (not from the bottle).

Confection:

Remove as much white skin as possible from the tangerine wedges. Also, remove the pits and cut them in half. In a saucepan, place the tangerine segments, sugar, and tangerine juice. Stir and cook over low heat for 1 hour and 10 minutes.

At the end, see if it has the desired consistency. Remove from the heat and place in sterilized jars.

Strawberry Jam

Ingredients: 750 g of strawberries, 750 g of sugar, 2 tablespoons of lemon juice.

Confection:

Cut the strawberries in half, as soon as they are washed and the stems removed, and place them in a pan. Stir in the lemon juice and sugar and cook, stirring occasionally, until the strawberries release their liquid.

Then increase the heat and, when it starts to boil, let it cook, stirring occasionally, for another 15 minutes. Remove from the heat and store in jars.

Apple and Cinnamon Compote

Ingredients: 2 kg of apple pieces, 1.6 kg of sugar, juice of 1 lemon, 2 cinnamon sticks.

Confection:

Place the apples in a bowl and drizzle them with lemon juice to keep them from oxidizing. In a wide pan, place the sugar, apple, and cinnamon sticks. Bring it to a boil and stir until the sugar dissolves.

When it comes to a boil, cook until the apple cubes are soft and the jam thickens (about 45 minutes to 1 hour). Divide the jam into jars, previously sterilized, and store them in a cool, dry place for about 6 months.

Plum jam

Ingredients: 1.5 kg of red plums, 1.5 kg of sugar, and 300 ml of water.

Confection:

Wash the plums very well, cut them in half and remove the pit. Place them in a pan with water, bring to the boil, and cook until the plums start to soften.

Remove the pan from the heat, add the sugar, and stir until the sugar is dissolved. Put the pan back on the heat and let it boil until it has the consistency of jam.

Pour the jam into sterilized glass jars and close them tightly. Store it in a dry and low-light place.

Carrot jam

Ingredients: 500 g of sugar, 500 g of peeled carrots, 1 lemon peel, 1 cinnamon stick.

Confection:

Bring the sugar, the carrots cut into small pieces, the lemon peel, and the cinnamon stick to the boil. Let it boil for about 6 minutes.

Discard the lemon peel and cinnamon stick and blend with a hand blender. Bring it to a simmer again and let it boil for another 6 minutes.

Place the jam in sterilized glass jars, close them, and turn them upside down until cool. Store it in a dark and dry place.

Sweet Tomato jam

Ingredients: 1.8 kg of skinless tomatoes, 400 ml of water, 2 lemons (the juice), and enough sugar.

Confection:

Cut the tomatoes into quarters, place them in a saucepan, add the lemon juice and water, and bring to a boil. Cover and boil for 40 minutes, until the tomato is very soft.

Measure the amount of tomato mixture you have obtained and weigh 450 g of sugar per 600 ml. Place the mixture and sugar in a saucepan, bring to the boil, and stir well until the sugar is dissolved.

Increase the intensity of the heat and let it boil for about 10 minutes, or until it reaches a temperature of 105° C (221 °F) with the kitchen thermometer.

Remove it from the heat and clean the surface of the candy with the help of a spoon (if there is foam). Place the jam in sterilized glass jars, close them and turn them upside down until they cool down. Store it in a dark and dry place.

Additional explanations

Stages of sugar boiling.

The names in Portuguese are different. Sorry if the translation is not accurate. In Portugal, we have at least 12 stages for sugar syrup.

Thread (or strands): boil for about 1 minute with 190 ml of water and 250 g of sugar at about 103° C (217 °F). The syrup starts to bubble up on the sides of the pan. It should run smoothly and smoothly, creating some grip on the spoon.

Strong Wire: sugar point with a temperature of 105° C (221 °F). It is especially used for fillings and jellies. If we put the syrup in a bowl with water, we can see that the thread is denser than the thread formed by the sugar syrup.

Soft ball, Pearl: with 120 ml of water and 250 g of sugar, at approximately 108° C (226 °F). Boil for about 4 minutes, until the thicker thread forms a small ball suspended at the end. If we put a little bit of the point in a bowl of water, it will form a point, similar to a pearl.

Road: 90 ml of water and 250 g of sugar at 110° C, boil for about 5 minutes. Dip your thumb and forefinger in cold water. If we put some sugar on a plate and divide it with a spoon into halves, the two halves will not come together, forming a "road" that lets you see the bottom.

Plow stage or fly: boil 60 ml of water and 250 g of sugar for 7 to 8 minutes at 117° C. Pass the skimmer in the syrup and blow, bubbles should form that burst quickly.

Sand: 50 ml of water and 250 g of sugar, at 140 ºC. The syrup starts to cling to the sides of the pan with a sandy consistency and starts to turn golden.

Caramel stage: 50 ml of water and 250 g of sugar, at 140° C. The syrup starts to turn into caramel, with a strong roasted aroma and a dark brown tone.

Sword stage: sugar point at 117° C, 60 ml of water for 250 g of sugar. It is the ideal spot to prepare camel drool or to crystallize fruit. When you drain the syrup with a fork, it will fall into slivers. If we put a little bit of the point on a fork, it will fall out looking like blades.

Candy stage: 50 ml of water and 250 g of sugar, sugar point at 129° C. Ideal for mirroring sweets. As soon as it comes into contact with cold water, it forms a hard, brittle mound.

Paste stage: 190 ml of water and 250 g of sugar, at 101° C, boil for 1 minute. Let it drain into the pan and if the syrup runs like water, the sugar has not yet reached its point. As soon as a small layer of sugar begins to adhere to the spoon, it is at the point of paste.

Bain Marie

Technically, the water bath consists of heating ingredients that cannot be exposed directly to the fire or that cannot boil. To make a bain-marie, you need to place the ingredients inside a container which, in turn, is placed inside another container (pot) containing hot or boiling water. In this way, the bain-marie allows you to melt, cook, or heat the ingredients slowly and evenly.

Sugar at Road stage

Thread

Hair Stitch

Soft ball, pearl stage

Blown or fly

Sand

Baking in Bain Marie

Author

Joana Lima

Joana is 39 years old and is from Esposende, in Braga, Portugal. She loves to cook and decided to publish two works: "Traditional Portuguese Dishes" and "Traditional Portuguese Sweets and Cakes", to share a little of Portuguese flavors and culture. She will soon publish her third book, on liqueurs.

Bibliography

Google searches.

teleculinaria.pt

pingodoce.pt

Recipessemenus.net

www.iguaria.com

www.mulherportuguesa.com

Traditional Portuguese Products: https://tradicional.dgadr.gov.pt

Book "Wonders of Confectionery". (anonymous).

www.receitasja.com